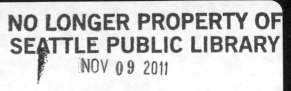

WEIRD HISTORY

A TWISTED TOUR

of America's Bizarre Past

by Matt Lake and Randy Fairbanks

STERLING CHILDREN'S BOOKS
New York

To Arnold Toynbee, the historian with the weirdest story ever —Matt
To my wife, Elizabeth, the girl at the front of the classroom —Randy

STERLING CHILDREN'S BOOKS
New York

An Imprint of Sterling Publishing
387 Park Avenue South
New York, NY 10016

ISBN 978-1-4027-6040-2

Library of Congress Cataloging-in-Publication Data

Lake, Matthew.
 Weird history : a twisted tour of America's bizarre past / by Matt Lake and Randy Fairbanks.
    p. cm.
  Includes index.
  ISBN 978-1-4027-6040-2
  1. Parapsychology--United States--History--Juvenile literature. 2. Occultism--United States--
History--Juvenile literature. I. Fairbanks, Randy. II. Title.
  BF1028.5.U6L35 2011
  001.90973--dc22

011011241

Distributed in Canada by Sterling Publishing
c/o Canadian Manda Group, 165 Dufferin Street
Toronto, Ontario, Canada M6K 3H6

Photography and illustration credits are found on page 127 and constitute an extension of this copyright page.

Designed by Anke Stohlmann Design.

For information about custom editions, special sales, premium and corporate purchases, please contact Sterling Special Sales
Department at 800-805-5489 or specialsales@sterlingpublishing.com.

Manufactured in China
Lot #: 10 9 8 7 6 5 4 3 2 1
07/11

This book is intended as entertainment to present a historical record of local legends, folklore, and sites throughout the United States
of America. Many of these legends and stories cannot be independently confirmed or corroborated, and the authors and publisher make
no representation as to their factual accuracy. The reader should be advised that some of the sites described in this book are located on
private property and should not be visited without permission, or you may face prosecution for trespassing.

www.sterlingpublishing.com/kids

CONTENTS

A MAGICAL HISTORY TOUR

to us, "weird" is the mystery of the unknown and the unexplainable. It's that little chill that gives you goose bumps or the unfamiliar sound emanating from the shadows that pricks up your ears. Sometimes it's the story that's so absurd and ridiculous, all you can do is laugh about it. Other times, it's the story that leaves you slightly frightened and ill at ease. Weird is the unique, the unusual, and the unexpected.

If history is a record and explanation of past events (and it is . . . we checked), weird history is a record of bizarre people, strange places, and odd events in which explanations aren't always possible. And since you can find regular old history in textbooks and encyclopedias, we here at Weird Central thought a book about the history of weirdness in the U.S. would be . . . well . . . weird (and fun!). Instead of presidents, wars, treaties, and important decisions, we give you America's first (and only) self-proclaimed emperor, the ghost of Abigail Adams doing the president's wash at the White House, aliens attacking New Jersey, secret societies, witches, ancient mysteries, and more!

Unlike those other history books, there are no dates to remember, and we doubt you'll ever be quizzed on the events that unfold in these pages. But don't be fooled! These are important historical moments, because without them we wouldn't be the weird and wonderful country that we are!

Weird Central

Before we take you on this magical history tour of the weirdest America has to offer, we should introduce ourselves. We're researchers and writers at Weird Central, a mysterious base (located somewhere in the swamps of Jersey) where news of all the weird things in the U.S. eventually ends up. Imagine a small, cramped office with phones ringing off the hooks; e-mails coming in by the thousands from correspondents from all fifty states checking in with new weird stories; and vast data banks of weirdness whirring and clicking with up-to-the-minute news of UFOs, hauntings, ghost ships, and sideshow heroes. Well, Weird Central is nothing like that, but we do collect these stories, and we've put the best of them in this book!

Step right up, ladies and gentlemen, the show's about to start. Come one, come all!

See page 66 to find out what Americans did for fun before TV!

Nobody calls the Emperor of America weird and gets away with it!

Want to help me with the wash? (See page 28!)

Did we miss your favorite story? Write to us and let us know. The weird will never run out completely, and we have plans to deliver it to you in a whole series of Weird U.S. books. Just watch and wait—and send us your stories! We know they're out there.

FAMOUS & WEIRD

just because you're on a ten-dollar bill, doesn't mean you're normal. And even if you're the commander in chief of a great nation, that doesn't preclude you from having a close encounter with aliens.

In fact, the more research we do into dusty old archives and the more old books and speeches we read, the more convinced we are that if your name is in the history books, you've got a lot of weird to go along with the bravery and smarts that got you remembered in the first place. We've dug up many stories of famous people, of course, but instead of their more famous exploits, we've found out about some of the weird things they have seen or done. And trust us, there's plenty of weirdness to go around!

I challenge you to a duel.

Peculiar Presidents

It takes a special kind of person to become president of the United States. You need great dedication, a strong personality, and, in several cases, a big helping of weirdness. In fact, when we dusted off our files on four past presidents, we discovered a lot more than legislation and heroic deeds, including UFOs, Bigfoot, psychic dreams, and more!

Two Sightings for the Gipper

Before he became the fortieth president of the United States, Ronald Reagan was the thirty-third governor of California. And before that, he was a movie star. His most famous line from the movies was, "Go out and win one for the Gipper," but in the 1970s, he went out and *saw* two for the Gipper—two UFOs, that is.

While he was governor of California, Ronald Reagan and his wife, Nancy, once showed up very late to a party at actor William Holden's house. Another of the guests, Lucille Ball, later wrote in her autobiography that when the Reagans finally arrived, they were both very excited and told everyone at the party that they had seen a UFO while driving down the highway. Lucille Ball wrote, "After he was elected president, I kept thinking about that event, and wondered if he still would have won if he told everyone that he saw a flying saucer."

We don't know about that, but he did tell a reporter about the *second* time he saw one. This was in 1974, while he was being flown in the governor's private airplane into Bakersfield, California. He told the Washington bureau chief of the *Wall Street Journal*, "It was a bright white light. We followed it to Bakersfield, and all of a sudden to our utter amazement, it went straight up into the heavens." The reporter checked out the story with the pilot of the plane, Air Force Colonel Bill Paynter, who said, "It appeared to be several hundred yards away . . . then the light took off. The UFO went from normal cruise speed to a fantastic speed instantly. If you give an airplane power, it will accelerate, but not like a hot rod, and that's what this was like. Governor Reagan expressed amazement. I told the others I didn't know what it was."

And we don't know what it was either. That's why they call these flying saucers Unidentified Flying Objects. But one thing's for sure: Ronald Reagan was not the only president to see one.

Was it a bird? A plane? A UFO?

Take Me to Your (Future) Leader

Jimmy Carter was president of the United States from 1977 to 1981, but a few years before, when he was governor of Georgia, he and ten other men saw something strange in the night sky outside a country club in Leary, Georgia. He often spoke about it, even at political events. A few years after the sighting, he told the Southern Governors' Conference, "It was the darndest thing I've ever seen. We watched it for ten minutes, but none of us could figure out what it was. One thing's for sure. I'll never make fun of people who say they've seen unidentified objects in the sky. If I become president, I'll make every piece of information this country has about UFO sightings available to the public and the scientists." As president, Carter had to be more careful about what he said (nobody wants to think their president is weird!), but he did make the CIA release to the public a lot of its files on UFO sightings.

If a UFO visits you, perhaps you'll grow up to be president one day— just like me!

I'll come back when you're president!

If you see a UFO, maybe you can fill out the same form that Governor Carter did for a UFO investigator! He described his UFO as very bright and about the size of the moon. It also changed colors and shapes.

International UFO Bureau
In Cooperation With Canadian UFO Report Magazine
P. O. Box 1281
OKLAHOMA CITY, OKLAHOMA 73103

SIGHTING Form
A-UFO REPORTS

1. NAME *Jimmy Carter*   PLACE OF EMPLOYMENT

   ADDRESS *State Capitol Atlanta*   OCCUPATION *Governor*

   EDUCATION *Graduate*   SPECIAL TRAINING *Nuclear Physics*   MILITARY SERVICE *US Navy*

   TELEPHONE *404-656-1776*

2. DATE OF OBSERVATION *Oct 1969*   TIME   AM   PM *7:15*   TIME ZONE *EST*

3. LOCALITY OF OBSERVATION *Leary, Georgia*

4. HOW LONG DID YOU SEE THE OBJECT?   HOURS *10-12* MINUTES   SECONDS

5. PLEASE DESCRIBE WEATHER CONDITIONS AND THE TYPE OF SKY; I.E., BRIGHT DAYLIGHT, NIGHTTIME, DUSK, ETC. *Shortly after dark*

6. POSITION OF THE SUN OR MOON IN RELATION TO THE OBJECT AND TO YOU. *Not in sight*

7. IF SEEN AT NIGHT, TWILIGHT, OR DAWN, WERE THE STARS OR MOON VISIBLE? *Stars*

8. WERE THERE MORE THAN ONE OBJECT? *No*   IF SO, PLEASE TELL HOW MANY, AND DRAW A SKETCH OF WHAT YOU SAW, INDICATING DIRECTION OF MOVEMENT, IF ANY.

9. PLEASE DESCRIBE THE OBJECT(S) IN DETAIL. FOR INSTANCE, DID IT (THEY) APPEAR SOLID, OR ONLY AS A SOURCE OF LIGHT; WAS IT REVOLVING, ETC? PLEASE USE ADDITIONAL SHEETS OF PAPER, IF NECESSARY.

10. WAS THE OBJECT(S) BRIGHTER THAN THE BACKGROUND OF THE SKY? *Yes*

11. IF SO, COMPARE THE BRIGHTNESS WITH THE SUN, MOON, HEADLIGHTS, ETC. *at one time bright as moon*

12. DID THE OBJECT(S) --   (PLEASE ELABORATE, IF YOU CAN GIVE DETAILS.)

    A: APPEAR TO STAND STILL AT ANY TIME? *yes*
    B: SUDDENLY SPEED UP AND RUSH AWAY AT ANY TIME?
    C: BREAK UP INTO PARTS OR EXPLODE?
    D: GIVE OFF SMOKE?
    E: LEAVE ANY VISIBLE TRAIL?
    F: DROP ANYTHING?
    G: CHANGE BRIGHTNESS? *yes*
    H: CHANGE SHAPE? *size*
    I: CHANGE COLOR? *yes*

    Seemed to move toward us from a distance, stop, move partially away, then depart. Bluish at first, then reddish, luminous, not solid.

13. DID THE OBJECT(S) AT ANY TIME PASS IN FRONT OF, OR BEHIND OF, ANYTHING? IF SO PLEASE ELABORATE GIVING DISTANCE, SIZE, ETC, IF POSSIBLE. *No*

14. WAS THERE ANY WIND? *No*   IF SO, PLEASE GIVE DIRECTION AND SPEED.

15. DID YOU OBSERVE THE OBJECT(S) THROUGH AN OPTICAL INSTRUMENT OR OTHER AID, WINDSHIELD, WINDOWPANE, STORM WINDOW, SCREENING, ETC? *No*   WHAT?

16. DID THE OBJECT(S) HAVE ANY SOUND? *No*   WHAT KIND?   HOW LOUD?

17. PLEASE TELL IF THE OBJECT(S) WAS (WERE) --
    A: FUZZY OR BLURRED.
    B: LIKE A BRIGHT STAR.
    C: SHARPLY OUTLINED. ✓

Lincoln's Visions

Almost every president says he has a vision or a dream. He usually means that he has an idea of how things ought to be. But in the case of Abraham Lincoln, he meant it literally. He had dreams and visions that foretold the future—or at least, that's what he and his wife believed.

The day he was elected president in 1860, Lincoln flopped down on a couch to take a rest and caught sight of himself in a mirror. He saw two images of his face—one was normal but the other was as pale as a ghost's. He told his wife about this, but when she came to the mirror, she didn't see it. When he looked at the mirror later, he saw the two images again. In the weeks and years that followed, the Lincolns came to believe that the pale and ghostly second image meant that he would serve only one term as president and die shortly afterward.

Things were tough for the Lincolns. Some of their children died young, and to add to their personal grief, the whole nation was at war with itself while Lincoln was president. As the war came to an end, Abe told his friend Ward Hill Lamon about a strange dream he had. Lamon wrote down the dream and published it later in a book he called *Recollections of Abraham Lincoln*. Here's how Abe described his dream:

I could not have been long in bed when I fell into a slumber, for I was weary. I soon began to dream. There seemed to be a death-like stillness about me. Then I heard subdued sobs, as if a number of people were weeping. I thought I left my bed and wandered downstairs. . . . "Who is dead in the White House?" I demanded of one of the soldiers, "The President," was his answer; "he was killed by an assassin." Then came a loud burst of grief from the crowd, which woke me from my dream.

Three days after he told Lamon his dream, Lincoln called his cabinet for a meeting. Nobody in the government had any idea that there was a plot to kill

the president that very night—except perhaps the president himself. As the members of the cabinet entered the room, they saw the president looking very serious. "Gentlemen, before long you will have important news," he told them. "I have had a dream. I have dreamed it three times before; once before the battle of Bull Run, once on another occasion, and again last night. I am in a boat, alone on a boundless ocean. I have no oars, no rudder. I am helpless. I drift!"

After making this strange speech, he continued the meeting as usual. But later that night, as he went to the theater, he said "good-bye" to his security guard, Colonel William Crook. It was the only time he had ever said the word *good-bye* to Colonel Crook—he always said "good night." The colonel thought it was strange at the time, because Lincoln was a good writer and speechmaker, and he chose his words very carefully. A few hours later, the president was shot while watching a play. All the people he had spoken to that day were convinced that he knew he would not survive. All these dreams and visions were telling him he would soon die. What do you think?

The Bigfoot President.

Teddy Roosevelt, the Bigfoot President

Theodore Roosevelt achieved many great things in his life. He is remembered today for establishing the National Forest Service, making treaties so that the Panama Canal could be built, and winning the Nobel Peace Prize. He's also one of the four presidents whose faces are carved on Mount Rushmore.

Roosevelt loved riding his horse, and before he became president he spent many months living with trappers and hunters in the wilderness. Ten years before he was president, he wrote a book about his experiences called *The Wilderness Hunter*; in it, he told a story about a wild creature that sounds an awful lot like Bigfoot. This was years before anybody used the word *Bigfoot*, of course. But Roosevelt had a much more dramatic way of describing him anyway: "half human or half devil, some great goblin-beast."

Roosevelt did not see Bigfoot himself, and the trapper who told him the story didn't get a clear look at him either. But the trapper—a man named Bauman— believed that some monster was following him and his friend in the badlands of the Dakota frontier. Bauman's friend may have gotten a better look at this creature, but he never told anybody about it. That's because the creature killed him. Roosevelt clearly believed his friend was trustworthy and expected his readers to make up their own minds about what really happened. So what do you think? Was Bauman just telling a spooky story to scare the young man who was destined to be president? Or did he really have a close encounter with Bigfoot?

The Bigfoot encounter, in President Roosevelt's own words:

Frontiersmen are not, as a rule, apt to be very superstitious. They lead lives too hard and practical, and have too little imagination in things spiritual and supernatural. . . . But I once listened to a goblin story which rather impressed me. It was told by a grisled, weather-beaten old mountain hunter, named Bauman. . . . He must have believed what he said, for he could hardly repress a shudder at certain points of the tale. . . . When the event occurred, Bauman was still a young man, and was trapping with a partner among the mountains. . . . They . . . reached a little open glade where they concluded to camp, . . . and after building a brush lean-to . . . they started up stream. . . . At dusk . . . they were surprised to find that . . . something, apparently a bear, . . . had rummaged about among their things, . . . destroying their lean-to. . . . The footprints of the beast were quite plain, [and his partner] remarked, "Bauman, that bear has been walking on two legs." . . . Upon again examining the tracks . . . , they certainly did seem to be made by but two paws, or feet. However, it was too dark to make sure. . . . The two men rolled up in their blankets, and went to sleep. . . .

At midnight Bauman was awakened by some noise, and . . . his nostrils were struck by a strong wild-beast odor, and he caught the loom of a great body in the darkness at the mouth of the lean-to. Grasping his rifle, he fired at the vague, threatening shadow, but must have missed, for immediately afterwards he heard the smashing of the underwood as the thing, whatever it was, rushed off. . . .

In the morning they started out. . . . By an unspoken agreement they kept together all day, and returned to camp towards evening. . . . The visitor . . . had returned, and in wanton malice had tossed about their camp kit and bedding, and destroyed the shanty. The ground was marked up by its tracks, and on leaving the camp it had gone along the soft earth by the brook, where the footprints were as plain as if on snow. . . . It had walked off on but two legs. The men . . . kept up a roaring fire throughout the night, one or the other sitting on guard most of the time.

About midnight the thing came down through the forest . . . and stayed there on the hill-side for nearly an hour. They could hear the branches crackle as it moved about, and several times it uttered a harsh, grating, long-drawn moan, a peculiarly sinister sound. Yet it did not venture near the fire. In the morning, [they] decided that they would shoulder their packs and leave the valley that afternoon. . . . At noon they were back within a couple of miles of camp. . . . Bauman volunteered to gather [traps] while his companion went ahead to camp and made ready the packs. . . . As he hurried towards camp under the tall trees, the silence and desolation of the forest weighed on him. . . . There was nothing to break the ghostly stillness. . . . At last he came to the edge of the little glade where the camp lay, and shouted as he approached it, but got no answer. The camp fire had gone out, though the thin blue smoke was still curling upwards. Near it lay the packs, wrapped and arranged. . . . Stepping forward he again shouted, and as he did so his eye fell on the body of his friend, stretched beside the trunk of a great fallen spruce. . . . The body was still warm, but . . . the neck was broken, while there were four great fang marks in the throat. The footprints of the unknown beast-creature, printed deep in the soft soil, told the whole story.

Weird Founding Father

Benjamin Franklin was a scientist, inventor, musician, publisher, and writer. During his life, he was famous across America and Europe for his clever inventions. His design for a wood-burning stove kept thousands of people alive in harsh winters, and his bifocal glasses are used even today. He was also a statesman who tried to make peace between Britain and its American colonies, and when he realized that would never happen, he sided with the colonies and boldly signed his name on the Declaration of Independence. But in addition to being an international hero, this Boston-born founding father from Philly could also be a tad odd.

Franklin loved electricity, and he would throw parties with what he called "electric bumpers"—drinking glasses that were wired to an old-fashioned type of battery, so that you'd get a shock on your lips when you took a sip. His idea of a great party was to invite people to watch him electrocute a turkey, which he would then have his cook prepare using an electric current—more than a hundred years before the invention of the electric oven. And he dreamed of generating enough electricity to send great arcs of current across Philadelphia's Schuylkill River, though he never managed to pull that off. The closest he came to seeing big sparks at a party was the time he electrocuted himself by accident. The batteries of the time had only enough charge for one good jolt, so the turkey went free that day. It may be a coincidence, but many years later when the Founding Fathers were trying to decide which bird to use as the symbol of the United States, Franklin was the only man not to vote for the bald eagle. Benjamin Franklin's choice for the American national bird was the turkey.

Not Politics as Usual

Sure, politicians enjoy arguing with each other, but can you imagine the vice president shooting the secretary of the treasury? Well, that's exactly what Vice President Aaron Burr did to Alexander Hamilton in 1804. Hamilton was an important member of President Thomas Jefferson's government and created the Federal Reserve Bank (which is why his face is on the front of the ten-dollar bill). Burr's term as VP was coming to an end and he was running for governor of New York. But Hamilton was just as ambitious, and he wrote some nasty things about Burr that turned the election against him. So Burr challenged Hamilton to a duel, which took place on July 11, 1804, in Weehawken, New Jersey.

Now, a duel wasn't a free-for-all gunfight but rather a formal way of defending your honor. The participants arrived unarmed and were handed guns by their friends. They walked to a fixed distance apart and faced each other. Most duelers just shot at the ground or into the air, as a symbol of defending their reputation, and waited for the opponent to do the same so they could both walk away with their honor intact. That's what Hamilton did; however, Burr's bullet hit Hamilton square in the torso. He died the following day.

Burr made a run for it and escaped to New Hope, Pennsylvania, and then the Carolinas. In New Hope, which today's residents call the most haunted town in America, Burr hid out in the cellar of a friend's house. The house still stands today, and in honor of its most notorious guest, it's now called the Aaron Burr House. Visitors believe it's haunted by the spirit of the scared VP. People speak of a cold wave washing over them and a strong sensation of being stared at. And at night, you can hear a furtive sound, like a killer on the run, creeping to avoid capture from enemies.

Um . . . wouldn't you rather arm wrestle? Or how about a rousing game of Frisbee golf?

The Wacky Inventions of Thomas Edison

Thomas Alva Edison helped shape the modern world. He invented more than a thousand new devices, including three of the most important things in our lives today: he's the man behind the first reliable electric lights, the first sound recordings, and the first movies. Edison also ran one of the earliest movie and sound recording studios that launched the modern entertainment industry. He said that his successes were because of his hard work: "ninety-nine percent perspiration, one percent inspiration" was his most famous line.

If that's true, imagine how he must have sweated over some of his less successful ventures.

Electric Eccentric

Thomas Edison's inventions ran on one kind of electricity—direct current—the kind that's used in battery-operated devices today. Edison wanted everyone to use only direct current (DC for short). But there's another kind of electricity, alternating current or AC, and when another inventor, George Westinghouse, began to sell AC appliances, Edison went into action. He told everybody—quite truthfully—that AC could kill you. The direct current that his inventions used, he said, was harmless. Westinghouse spoiled Edison's fun by admitting that AC could kill you—but so could dynamite and whiskey, and they were safe if you used them carefully. So Edison was forced to go into overdrive. He demonstrated the dangers of AC by electrocuting animals in his lab in West Orange, New Jersey. Unfortunately, the New York State police were looking for a humane way to execute people, and they thought that electrocution would do nicely. So beginning in 1890, they used the electric chair to execute prisoners.

When his first demonstrations didn't work, Edison made another attempt to scare people off AC. An elephant at Coney Island, New York, was condemned to death for killing three people, and Edison offered to electrocute the animal. He pushed 6,600 volts of AC through him and filmed the event with his movie cameras. He then distributed the short film, *Electrocuting an Elephant*, in 1903. Edison was sure this would put people off the idea of alternating current forever, but it had the opposite effect. The power of AC impressed everyone. That's why today we have AC in our home's electrical sockets, running Westinghouse brand appliances. But Edison had his way, too: we use DC in our flashlights and iPods.

Edison made Topsy go turvy in an over-the-top demonstration attempting to prove AC was dangerous.

Edison Hears Dead People

In his constant quest to invent new things, Edison took some strange turns. In 1878, he hit upon the idea of communicating with the dead. He came across a group called the Theosophists who believed that human intelligence carried on after death and migrated into new bodies. It's a theory called reincarnation, which many Eastern religions also believe in.

Edison came up with a scientific way to explain how reincarnation could work: the human mind might be based on particles that floated away after the body died and drifted into new bodies by some force like magnetism or gravity. And he thought that if he could build a machine to trap these particles, he could talk to the dead. It's an interesting idea, perhaps, but he never managed to figure out how to do it.

You can visit Thomas Edison's lab in Menlo Park, New Jersey.

Edison Reads Your Mind

Another great businessman of Edison's day, the motor manufacturer Henry Ford, introduced Edison to another idea—reading people's minds. Edison visited a fortune-teller and thought he might be able to make the electrical signals in the brain strong enough to transmit to another person's brain. He experimented with wrapping electrical coils around his own head and the heads of his guests. We're glad we weren't around to be invited into Edison's telepathy machine. If it failed, we wouldn't want to see a great inventor embarrassed. And if it did work, he would know exactly how silly we thought his idea was.

HAUNTED BY HISTORY

a few years ago, during one of our Weird road trips, we stopped at a small town and took a walking tour of local haunted landmarks. Along the way, we noticed something strange. We kept bumping into another tour group: the Happy History Buff Tour. At first, the history buffs didn't want to mingle with the ghost hunters; however, by the end of the tour, we were one big group exploring the past together. This got us wondering. Why were all of the historic landmarks haunted? Do history and ghosts somehow go together? "Ask the ghost tour guy," replied the history buff tour guide when we asked him these questions. "Ask the history guy," replied the ghost tour guide.

Since then we've noticed the same phenomena in other towns across the country: the historical walking tours and the ghost walking tours always go to the same places. This makes life a little easier for those of us who consider ourselves both history buffs AND ghost hunters. And if you like your history peppered with ghosts and spirits, you should enjoy this tour we've put together for you. Welcome to the historical haunted landmarks of Weird America.

Empire State Ghosts

When it was finished in 1931, the Empire State Building in New York City was the most magnificent skyscraper in the world. At 103 stories tall and more than 1,450 feet high, it quickly became a hotspot for people contemplating ending it all by jumping off the building. The situation only got worse after moviegoers saw the 1933 film *King Kong*. Anyone familiar with the movie will remember how it ends: King Kong climbs to the top of the Empire State Building. Planes swarm around him and he swats at them. Finally, injured by machine-gun fire, he loses his grip. Then he falls . . .

Sixteen people hurled themselves from the observatory on the eighty-sixth floor of the Empire State Building during the 1930s and 1940s. Finally, in December 1947, a fence was installed around the observation platform, and most jumpers have since been discouraged. According to legend, a few of these sad souls continue to haunt the skyscraper. Wispy forms have appeared in photos taken on the observatory, and many witnesses have reported ghost sightings. Their accounts are surprisingly consistent. In each report, the witness glimpsed a figure running at the fence.

The view from eighty-six floors up!

Then, before their eyes, the specter passed through the wire mesh, to disappear into thin air. The spirits seem to be caught in a loop, eternally replaying the last moments of their lives. One ghost is supposedly the girlfriend of a soldier who died during World War II. Some visitors have seen her crying in the women's restroom, wearing an outfit from the 1940s. Others have seen her reenacting her leap. Has anyone ever seen the ghost of King Kong? Well, no . . . the great ape's a fictional character, remember? And we've never heard of anyone spotting the ghost of a made-up monster. That would be too weird, even for us!

Wyatt Earp and his Tombstone pals.

The Gunfight at the O.K. Corral

The most famous gunfight in the history of the American West took place at the O.K. Corral in Tombstone, Arizona, on October 26, 1881. If you visit the "O.K. Corral Gunfight Site" in Tombstone, you'll see mannequins set up to illustrate exactly where everyone involved was standing and exactly where some of them died. You might even catch a live reenactment by actors in cowboy garb, and during the performance, they'll show you exactly what happened. Except, there are a few problems. For one thing, the "O.K. Corral Gunfight Site" isn't really the site of the O.K. Corral gunfight.

The actual shootings took place in a vacant lot nearby on Fremont Street. Another problem is that no one really knows *exactly* what happened at O.K. Corral. People disagree about even the most basic elements of the story. Were the good guys really good? Were the bad guys really bad?

According to the legend, the heroes were Doc Holliday and the Earp brothers, Virgil, Morgan, and Wyatt. And supposedly the bad guys were Billy Claiborne, Frank and Tom McLaury, and Ike and Billy Clanton. They were part of a group of ranchers known as "The Cowboys," and rumors abounded that some of these ranch hands were cattle rustlers and stagecoach robbers.

Virgil Earp was the city marshal at the time, and he'd deputized his brother Morgan. In an effort to clean up Tombstone, they began giving the Cowboys a hard time, citing them for disorderly behavior and for carrying firearms within the limits of the town. The intensity of the run-ins between the Earps and the Cowboys grew until the showdown on that autumn day in 1881. The shooting lasted for only about thirty seconds, and when it was over, Billy Clanton and the McLaury brothers were dead. Doc Holliday and Virgil and Morgan Earp were wounded, and Wyatt Earp walked away without a scratch.

In many movies, Wyatt Earp and his brothers have been portrayed as brave lawmen, while the Cowboys have been presented as brutes. However, some historians are convinced that the Earps were trying to gain power in Tombstone, which put them at odds with Sheriff Johnny Behan, who was known to be friendly with the Cowboys. Supporting this claim is a well-known fact that Ike Clanton and Tom McLaury weren't armed. Also, witnesses later claimed that, before guns were drawn, Billy Clanton cried out, "Don't shoot me. I don't want to fight."

The body of Billy Clanton is buried in Tombstone in the Boothill Graveyard. It's rumored that he rises from his grave at night and continues down the road, walking toward the O.K. Corral. Also, some visitors have come away with tales about ghostly men in cowboy hats who vanish into thin air. Many believe that these apparitions were the restless souls of Billy Claiborne, the Clantons, and the McLaurys. Were these men villains or victims? Were Wyatt Earp and his brothers heroes or cold-blooded murderers? These unanswerable questions only add to the mystery behind the legendary gunfight at the O.K. Corral.

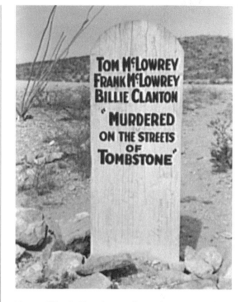

Terry "Ike" Clanton, a fourth-generation cousin of Ike Clanton, believes he's located the remains of Ike Clanton and hopes to bury his distant cousin at Boothill beside the graves of the other Cowboys.

If you visit Tombstone and witness a reenactment of the gunfight, you might feel a strange chill in the air, and you might be tempted to pinch the actors, just to make sure that they're alive.

Spooky house.

The Haunted House of the Seven Gables

There are two houses known as "The House of the Seven Gables." One is fictional; the other is real. But sometimes the line between fiction and reality can be very thin. . . . The fictional house comes from a book written by Nathaniel Hawthorne in 1851—*The House of the Seven Gables*—which horror writer H. P. Lovecraft considered "New England's greatest contribution to weird literature." In the novel, old Colonel Pyncheon obtains Matthew Maule's estate by wrongly accusing the man of witchcraft. "God will give him blood to drink," cries Maule just before dying. These words are the beginning of a terrible curse against the Pyncheon family. From that moment onward, an atmosphere of doom hangs heavy over the House of the Seven Gables.

In this terrifying tale about a cursed house, Hawthorne used elements from his own family history. His great-grandfather was one of the judges who participated in the Salem witch trials (see It's Witchcraft! on page 76). Also, Hawthorne modeled the house in the story on an actual house that he knew very well—the Ingersoll-Turner mansion, which was the home of his cousin Susan Ingersoll. Built in 1668, the Ingersoll-Turner House in Salem, Massachusetts, is older than any other wooden mansion in North America. Since it was the inspiration behind the book, the mansion has inherited the name "The House of the Seven Gables." And like its fictional counterpart, it seems to be haunted by the past.

Paranormalists have detected an aura of sadness that hangs over the steps in front of the house. Some have also heard the distant sounds of sobbing. They say that these are the cries of Nathaniel Hawthorne's mother, who never recovered from her husband's death at sea. Nathaniel Hawthorne's ghost is also rumored to reside there. Visitors have spotted him and his cousin Susan in

"Stealthy horror and disease lurk within the weather-blackened, moss-crusted, and elm-shadowed walls of the archaic dwelling." —*H. P. Lovecraft, describing the House of the Seven Gables*

Spooky author.

the first-story windows. The House of the Seven Gables is a weird place where fact, fiction, folklore, and history collide. It's a haunted house haunted by a haunted house, and if that doesn't make your head spin, then your head is probably on too tight.

The Search for Benjamin Franklin's Ghost

Ghost hunters and history buffs feel especially at home in Philadelphia, Pennsylvania. The city was chosen to be our nation's capital in 1774, long before Washington, D.C. was founded. A vital meeting place in the years preceding the American Revolution, Philadelphia has since become a vital meeting place for paranormalists. Most of them come to the City of Brotherly Love hunting one ghost in particular—the spirit of Benjamin Franklin. One of our Founding Fathers, Ben Franklin was a famous scientist and satirist, known for penning lines like, "In this world, nothing is certain but death and taxes." In keeping with the man's wit and mischievous streak, it's not surprising that the search for the ghost of Benjamin Franklin is full of red herrings and dead ends.

Boo!

The first stop on our ghost hunt was the house in which Franklin lived. We'd heard of other ghosts returning to the comfort of their homes, so why not Benjamin Franklin? To our surprise, the house turned out not to be a house at all—just a steel frame where a house used to be. Built in honor of Benjamin Franklin, it's called a "ghost structure." But that's the only thing ghostly about it. (What self-respecting ghost would haunt an empty steel frame shaped like a house?) Next, we visited an exhibit at the PECO Energy Liberty Center called "Benjamin Franklin's Ghost." An exhibit where people line up to meet a ghost? It seemed too good to be true. It turned out to be a holographic video image of the beloved Founding Father, which answered questions about American history. It was cool and very informative, but not in the least bit spooky.

In Bensalem, Pennsylvania, about twenty miles outside of Philadelphia, we visited Grouden Manor, which was once the home of Benjamin Franklin's cousin. It was here that Franklin supposedly gave his famous kite a few test runs. And some locals insist that the place is haunted by a mysterious man with a kite. Perhaps it's the ghost of Benjamin Franklin. Or maybe it's another ghost who enjoys flying kites. In any case, our search was getting more interesting. We returned to Philadelphia to explore Library Hall at the American Philosophical Society. This turned out to be the most promising stop on our Franklin ghost tour. The society was started by Ben Franklin in 1743, and the library contains a huge collection of books on the sciences and humanities. We learned a tale from the 1880s about a cleaning woman who insisted that she crashed into Benjamin Franklin's ghost amidst the stacks in the library. Apparently, the spirit was so preoccupied with his research that he didn't see her.

Also, we heard of another ghost legend involving a statue of Benjamin Franklin in front of Library Hall. If you visit the statue you might be surprised by what Ben's wearing. It's a toga! No, he wasn't taking part in an early American toga party. He wanted to be presented this way because he saw a connection between America and the republics of ancient Greece and Rome. Some witnesses claim that they've seen this statue come to life, and Benjamin Franklin sometimes jumps down from the perch, dances around in the streets, and heads off to hang out at the local pubs. (The ghost of Benjamin Franklin dancing around in a toga—now, that's scary!)

This statue looks like it's ready to get down and party!

A Ghost Tour of Washington, D.C.

Washington, D.C., was founded on July 16, 1790. In order to obtain the land for its capital, the newly formed U.S. government negotiated with local landowners, including one extremely stubborn Scottish gentleman named David Burns. George Washington called Burns "obstinate." Others called him "crusty." Well, after his death, Burns became an obstinate and crusty ghost. Of all of the ghosts that are reported to haunt Washington, D.C., David Burns came first. How do witnesses know they've encountered the ghost of David Burns? Simple! He announces himself by helpfully whispering, "I'm David Burns."

Many ghosts have followed in Burns's footsteps. Spirits of famous politicians and shades of unknown laborers are said to haunt our nation's capital. As far as we're concerned, there's no place in America where ghosts and history are more intertwined. To prove this point, we're taking you on a ghost tour of Washington, D.C. And while you're strolling along, if you hear a voice whisper, "I'm David Burns," don't be frightened. Just calmly reply, "Hello, Mr. Burns. How's life? . . . Oops, I mean . . . how's death?"

The Library of Congress

Filling three buildings on Capitol Hill, the Library of Congress (LOC) has more books than any other library in the world (more than 32 million!). Needless to say, it's easy to get lost in the stacks. But if you do, there's no need to worry. They say that a friendly ghost police officer patrols the premises and will be happy to help you find your way to the exit. We've also heard tales about doors closing by themselves, as well as mysterious banging noises coming from the stairwell. It sounds like the door-slamming, stair-thumping ghosts of the LOC must keep the librarians very busy. *Shhhhhh!*

Shhhhhh!

Meigs used more than 15.5 million bricks, and it's said that he made sure that every single brick was accounted for. (Whew! You try counting to 15,500,000!) When the building was finished in the 1890s, the reaction around Washington was not very positive. In fact, detractors often called it Meigs's Old Red Barn.

Nowadays, it's a museum devoted to the art of architecture and construction work in America. And its grand hall is often used as a ballroom for celebrating presidential inaugurations. These posh events attract all sorts of party crashers, and not all of them are made of flesh and blood. Visitors have seen hovering phantom faces swirling around the columns of the grand hall, seventy-five feet above the ground. Other witnesses have spotted a mysterious soldier riding a horse and swinging his sword. This ghostly presence is thought to be the spirit of General Meigs. Is he so proud of his creation that he can't bear to leave it behind? Or is he still counting bricks? We can't say for sure, but if you visit the National Building Museum, don't refer to it as Meigs's Old Red Barn. If you do, don't be surprised if you feel the gentle tap of a phantom sword on your shoulder . . .

The National Building Museum

General Montgomery C. Meigs, an engineer who supervised the construction of the dome of the U.S. Capitol, was also responsible for the colossal brick wonder now called the National Building Museum.

The White House

"I'm David Burns."

. . . Did you hear something? . . . Nah. . . .

The White House is said to be the favorite haunt of crusty and obstinate old Mr. Burns. Apparently, it's also inhabited by a long list of deceased presidents and family members.

Abigail Adams was the First Lady of the second president of the United States, John Adams. She was also the first First Lady to live in the White House AND the first phantom First Lady to haunt the place. They say that she can sometimes be seen hanging laundry in the East Room.

The Rose Garden at 1600 Pennsylvania Avenue is protected by the ghost of another first lady—Dorothea Dandridge Payne Todd "Dolley" Madison, the wife of the fourth U.S. president, James Madison. Dolley Madison planted the garden in the early 1800s, and it seems that she doesn't like people messing with it. One famous story about Dolley's ghost occurred more than sixty years after her death. President Woodrow Wilson's wife ordered gardeners to dig up the rosebushes. Dolley's ghost appeared and scolded the men, insisting that they leave her garden alone. The frightened men ran away, leaving Dolley's roses intact. Today, the rose garden blooms every summer

Laundry time!

Leave my roses alone!

just as it did two hundred years ago.

Over the years, there have been dozens of spooky encounters between living and dead first families. Mary Todd Lincoln was convinced that, more than once, she had heard the ghost of America's seventh president, Andrew Jackson, stomping and swearing in the Rose Room. It had been used as the presidential bedroom throughout Jackson's term, and so the ghost must have felt quite at home.

In later years, the Rose Room became known as the Queen's Bedroom because it was where the Queen of England slept during her White House visits. We've never heard stories about the Queen of England bumping into President Andrew Jackson's ghost, but there is a legendary tale about another queen and another ghost. One night while Franklin Delano Roosevelt was in office (1933–1945), Queen Wilhelmina of the Netherlands was sleeping in the Rose Room when a noise woke her up. Someone was knocking lightly on her door. Thinking that she was

The Queen's Bedroom.

being summoned because of an emergency, she raced to the door and swung it open. Outside, she saw the figure of a man who had been dead for more than sixty years. It was Abraham Lincoln! Queen Wilhelmina fainted, and when she came to, the ghost was gone.

In fact, of all the White House ghosts, Abraham Lincoln is the busiest. "I see him in different rooms and in the halls," said President Theodore Roosevelt. Grace Coolidge, the wife of President Calvin Coolidge, encountered Lincoln in the room that he had once used as a library—the Yellow Oval Room. Susan Ford, the daughter of President Gerald Ford, was so terrified of running into Lincoln's ghost that she refused to enter Lincoln's Bedroom, and she nervously referred to the sleeping chamber as "that room." Maureen

Reagan, the daughter of President Ronald Reagan, spent several nights in "that room" with her husband, Dennis Revell. The couple claimed that Lincoln's ghost had appeared to them as "an aura, sometimes red, sometimes orange." Many people believe that Abraham Lincoln's ghost only appears during times of crisis, like a guardian angel. Others say that Lincoln simply doesn't realize he's dead. So he wanders the halls of the White House, forever fretting over the problems of 1865, the year when he was assassinated. We offer a third theory, which is every bit as unbelievable as the first two. And it involves another well-known White House spirit.

In early 1862, the president's eleven-year-old son, Willie Lincoln, contracted an illness, probably typhoid fever. Weeks later, he died. "It is hard, hard to have him die,"

said the brokenhearted president. Hoping to contact Willie, Lincoln began attending séances. He became obsessed with his son's death, and some psychics feel that this obsession made it impossible for Willie to rest. In other words, Willie became a ghost so that he could be near his father. The ghost of Willie Lincoln has been seen many times in the White House, usually in the bedrooms on the second floor. Now, of course, all of this is very far-fetched, and you shouldn't believe a word of it, but if Willie became a ghost to be near his father, isn't it possible that President Lincoln might have become a ghost to be near his son? Perhaps Abraham Lincoln haunts the White House so that Willie Lincoln won't be lonely.

Willie Lincoln.

The U.S. Capitol Building

The final stop on our ghost tour is the U.S. Capitol. Ghost for ghost, it's a contender for the most haunted landmark in Washington, D.C. In fact, we can't think of any other building anywhere that has a weirder crew of phantom inhabitants.

John Quincy Adams was the son of John and Abigail Adams, and served as the sixth president of the United States. After his term ended, he remained a congressman for the last seventeen years of his life. On February 21, 1848, he suffered a stroke while making a speech in the House Chamber of the Capitol, and died two days later at the age of eighty-one.

Rumor has it that he's never left the building and is still trying to finish his speech. If you visit the Capitol and you're lucky enough to spot John Quincy Adams, please tell him to stop filibustering and go visit his dead mother at the White House. She's been hanging laundry for more than two hundred years and could use some help (see page 28).

America's twentieth president, James Garfield, is part of the ghostly crew, along with another man named Charles Julius Guiteau. Guiteau assassinated Garfield in 1881, after the president had served only six months in office. The story goes that they're locked in an eternal game of cat and mouse.

The ghost of John Quincy Adams need only walk about a mile and a half to help his mother with the laundry.

Garfield and Guiteau: two spirits caught in an endless game of cat and mouse.

Vice President Henry Wilson caught a chill after taking a dip in the Capitol hot tub. He died of pneumonia in November 1875 but can still be heard coughing, sneezing, and sniffling. Some visitors to the Capitol have detected the smell of bath soap lingering in the air.

Other shades in the U.S. Capitol include a mysterious stonemason who was accidentally sealed up within the basement walls. Trowel in hand, he stumbles through the subterranean passages, hoping to find a way out. And members of the Capitol maintenance team have reported strange encounters with a ghost janitor. They've heard eerie noises at night: water sloshing, buckets clanking. Some even claim to have seen a mop cleaning the floor by itself, pushed back and forth by invisible hands.

Still, there's another ghost at the Capitol terrifying enough to make you forget all the others. Yes, even scarier than the sneezing ghost of a politician! More frightening than the phantom mopper! No, it's not David Burns. This specter—with claws, sharp teeth, and a nasty temper—is known on Capitol Hill as the Demon Cat.

The legend of the Demon Cat begins soon after the Capitol was built, in the late 1700s. Supposedly, some of our founding fathers and the staff of the building were a bit sloppy about cleaning up after themselves. The leftover food attracted rats, and by the early 1800s the place was infested. Workmen decided to use cats to kill the rats. The idea worked, but it led to a spooky conclusion that no one could have predicted. After the rodent population dwindled, the cats were relieved of their mousing duties. Some were adopted as pets. Others became D.C. alley cats. But one creepy feline remained

behind and became a local legend. Is the Demon Cat a ghost from the Capitol's original rat patrol? Or is it an immortal creature with supernatural powers? No one really knows. But those who have encountered the monster have never forgotten the experience.

One security guard had a horrifying run-in with the Demon Cat on a chilly January evening in the 1970s. The guard was making his rounds in the dark basement and sub-basements underneath the Capitol. In a gray, gloomy passageway, he noticed movement out of the corner of his eye. A black cat! The animal approached him slowly, like a tiger stalking its prey. And as it came closer, the man could see that it was getting bigger and bigger. With each step, the Demon Cat grew until it was the size of a panther. The beast growled and reared back, preparing to strike. Baring its claws, it let out a deafening roar and pounced. The guard froze, waiting for the attack. But it never came. Suddenly, he was alone in the dark, silent hallway. The Demon Cat had disappeared. Okay, a cat that can grow and shrink and live forever is undeniably impressive. But we haven't gotten to the Demon Cat's most famous talent—its uncanny gift for prophecy. Supposedly, its appearance predicts changes in administration at the Capitol. Politicians, afraid of losing their jobs, pray that they never see the fabled beast. Also, it's rumored that the Demon Cat is a harbinger of doom. For example, we've heard that it was seen just before the stock market crash of 1929. And the assassination of President John F. Kennedy came right after another sighting in 1963. Evil cats and bad luck? Sounds like an old superstition, doesn't it? Still, every time we visit the U.S. Capitol, we can't help looking for its resident monster. So far, we've never spotted the Demon Cat, and we hope we never do.

A HISTORY OF VILLAINY

One way to look at our past is to count all the heroic deeds done by our great leaders, brilliant inventors, and brave soldiers. But if one part of history is about all the good guys, there has to be another side that's about all the bad guys. Here at Weird Central, we're always looking for villains to boo at. Some of them are kind of funny, while others are just plain scary. As we checked through our Weird files, we even found a villain or two who may not be quite so bad after all. We'll let you decide for yourself whether all the villains in this rogues' gallery deserve the title. One thing's for sure—history wouldn't be the same without them.

A hatchet was found at the scene of the murder of Andrew and Abby Borden; however, police never took fingerprints! It was a relatively new technology and local law-enforcement officials didn't trust it.

Lizzie Borden Took an Ax

Lizzie Borden took an ax
And gave her mother forty whacks.
And when she saw what she had done,
She gave her father forty-one.

This gruesome playground chant is about a real-life woman named Lizzie Borden, whose father and stepmother were killed more than a hundred years ago. The tale opens on August 4, 1892, at the Borden house in Fall River, Massachusetts. Five people lived there: the elderly Mr. Andrew Borden; his wife, Abby Borden; Mr. Borden's two daughters from his first marriage (Emma was forty-one years old and Lizzie was thirty-two); and Maggie, their maid. The family had been terribly sick—probably from eating fish that had gone bad in the heat—but there was something more than a case of jelly belly in the house when Lizzie came storming down the stairs and shouted, "Come down quick! Father's dead! Somebody's come in and killed him."

Two neighbors were contacted, and they found Mr. and Mrs. Borden dead in their rooms—killed by an ax. (The bit in the rhyme about forty whacks is bogus. Doctors who examined the bodies reckon the number was less than half that.) The following week, Lizzie Borden was arrested for murder. Almost immediately, people took sides. Lizzie was a popular woman around town. She was active in the Christian Endeavor Society and the Ladies Fruit and Flower Mission. She taught Sunday school and was a member of the Women's Christian Temperance Union. How could a woman like that kill anyone? People on the other side of the case said that she hated her father and her stepmother. Mr. Borden was a mean and cheap man, and Lizzie's stepmother was bossy and didn't care for either of her husband's daughters. The case was so sensational that newspapers across the country covered it closely. And that's about the time that kids began chanting the jump-rope rhyme.

The case of Lizzie Borden is still a bit of a mystery. The jury found her not guilty, and she went on to live a full life in Fall River—though she did move out of the Borden house. But many people who studied the case still suspect that Lizzie Borden did it and that the jury only let her off because they didn't want to give the death penalty to a woman.

The Lizzie Borden house in Fall River, Massachusetts.

Doting daughter or ax murderer?

35

The Innocent Men of the Wild West

Anyone who's ever seen a Western movie knows that the sheriff's job was to keep the bad guys at bay. That's what made the sheriff of Bannack, Montana, such an evil man. He did exactly the opposite. Henry Plummer breezed into town in 1862 and quickly impressed the townsfolk with his good manners and clean-cut appearance. He was such a perfect gentleman that in less than a year, the town elected him sheriff, which was when he brought his posse of thieves and murderers into town. They had been plotting to take over the town for a year, and Sheriff Plummer was actually the ringleader of this nasty gang of cutthroats!

Things went bad in Bannack almost immediately. Under the new lawman, a hundred people were killed within the first five months. And whenever townsfolk brought members of Plummer's gang to the sheriff's office, the bad guys would proclaim, "I am innocent" and be released right away. This plea eventually became the gang's nickname: the Innocents.

This reign of terror went on all summer and fall. Then Sheriff Plummer went too far and killed one of the most popular men in town. The townsfolk then formed their own gang, the Montana Vigilantes, and hunted down the murderers. Like the men who had terrorized, the Vigilantes showed no mercy. They caught the Innocents one by one and hanged them. In two weeks, they had dispensed summary justice on twenty-four men, and the rest of the gang fled. The Vigilantes finally found Plummer, and even though he wept and begged for mercy, he got the same punishment he had delivered to so many truly innocent people—the death penalty.

Bannack is now a ghost town and state park. You can visit the empty buildings, including the jailhouse where the sheriff abused the good people of the town.

Hetty Green, the Witch of Wall Street

There are lots of mean people in the world, but it takes a *really* mean person to get into *Guinness World Records* as the greatest miser the world has ever known. Only one person has ever earned that dubious honor: Hetty Green of New Bedford, Massachusetts, a woman so rich and so horrible that everyone called her the Witch of Wall Street.

Hetty Green was born rich (her family owned a large whaling fleet), but in 1865, she became *spectacularly* rich when she inherited from two relatives nearly $10 million—which back then was like having $185 million. Instead of buying a new house or some clothes, Hetty became obsessed with making her fortune grow. To her, that meant not spending any money at all if she could help it. She owned only one black dress and wore the same underwear every day, and she and her son lived in run-down boardinghouses, where Hetty spent her days clipping coupons and eating cold oatmeal. But it gets worse. When her son injured his knee, instead of paying for a doctor, she dressed him in ragged clothes and took him to a free clinic. When the staff realized that she was the famously rich Hetty Green, they refused to treat her son without payment. She didn't spend the money, and eventually, her son's leg had to be amputated. You can't get any meaner than that!

Hetty's meanness eventually killed her. In 1916, she was screaming at her maid for buying whole milk instead of the cheaper skimmed milk when she keeled over and died. She left behind a fortune worth more than $100 million (nearly $1.5 billion in today's dollars).

Don't tell anyone but I'm wearing my Tuesday underwear . . . and it's Friday!

37

The Secret Life of Doctor Wilson

Way back in 1818, a stranger arrived in Dummerston, Vermont. After kicking around for a few years, he offered to build the nearby town of Brookline its own schoolhouse and act as schoolteacher. He was a bit eccentric—he always wore a scarf around his neck and was a little wobbly on his legs. He used to lose his balance and fall down a lot. But he was smart and charming and, better yet, he was also a doctor. And if there's one thing a little New England town needed, it was someone who could be their schoolteacher *and* doctor.

So the town took him up on his offer, and Dr. John Wilson spent nearly thirty years in the area. By the time of his death in 1847, he was considered a local hero. When he knew he would soon die, he gathered his friends and asked them to bury him fully clothed, including his scarf. It was an odd request, but they agreed. However, nobody told the undertaker about it, and when he prepared the body for burial, he found that Dr. Wilson's neck was badly scarred, one of his legs had a bullet hole in it, and instead of a heel, one of his feet had a big lump of cork.

The sheriff was brought in to investigate. He studied a list of all the criminals who had been missing since the year Dr. Wilson came to town, and he found the perfect match: an Irish highwayman named John Doherty. This notorious criminal used to rob people as they traveled through Ireland and the border between Scotland and England. He appeared out of nowhere, took money and valuables, and disappeared into thin air. He was so fast that he earned the nickname Captain Thunderbolt. He had escaped from the law in Britain in 1818 along with his partner in crime, another Irishman named Michael Martin, who used the nickname Captain Lightfoot.

Captain Thunderbolt to the rescue!

Lightfoot was captured for other crimes in 1821 in Springfield, Massachusetts, and made a full confession to all his crimes because he wanted to escape the death penalty. He told the authorities that he and Captain Thunderbolt had committed all these crimes in Britain before emigrating, and told them all about Doherty's scars and fake heel. But the authorities didn't make any deal with Lightfoot, and they hanged him anyway. His description of Captain Thunderbolt stayed in police files for more than twenty years, but because he wasn't using his real name, Doc Wilson—er . . . we mean John Doherty . . . was never taken into custody.

So Doc Wilson, who had been a model citizen, was not a citizen or a doctor or even John Wilson. He was a fugitive from justice. But he left behind a monument to his good side.

The ROUND SCHOOLHOUSE

Designed -1821- By Dr. John "Thunderbolt" Wilson.
Built in 1822 on this site deeded to the Town of Brookline by Peter Benson, for the sum of $5.00
Dr. Wilson a former Scottish highwayman, taught the first term of 60 pupils who sat on benches.
The interior was completely renovated in 1910 and on March 5 1929 the building was turned over to the Town of Brookline for use as the town hall.
This building is thought to be the only round schoolhouse ever constructed in this country.

If you visit Brookline, Vermont, you can see the round schoolhouse he designed in 1821, the year his sidekick was executed. It's a strange and fun red-brick building, with windows facing all directions. The question is this: were those windows designed to give the students enough light to read, or were they to give the "doctor" a good view of any approaching policemen? We'll never know.

Typhoid Mary is known to have infected fifty-three people, three of whom died.

Typhoid Mary

Mary Mallon was a cook who made people so sick that some of them died—but it wasn't from her cooking. She had a strange secret that almost nobody back then could figure out. The secret cast her as a famous villain known as Typhoid Mary, although many doubt she even understood what was happening.

The story of Typhoid Mary started in 1907, when a wealthy New York banker named Charles Warren took his family to Long Island to vacation. His daughter fell ill with typhoid fever; soon, five more of the eleven people in the house had contracted the disease. One of the healthy members was their cook, Mary Mallon. The man who rented Mr. Warren his vacation home was scared that his house had made them ill. So he hired an engineer named George Soper to investigate. Soper traced every single lead he could find, including the employment history of the staff at the house. He found that between 1900 and 1907, every house where Mary Mallon had worked suffered outbreaks of typhoid. Mr. Soper knew that if Miss Mallon was infected with typhoid and didn't wash her hands properly before preparing food, she could have passed the disease to everyone.

Mr. Soper tried to get a blood sample from Mary, but she grabbed a carving knife and chased him off. And in some ways, who can blame her? Imagine what you would do if a complete stranger came up to you and said, "You don't wash your hands and that habit has killed people. Let's stick this needle in you." Soper called in the police and doctors from the New York City Health Department. Mary escaped over a fence, but they caught and tested her. She did have typhoid, but she seemed healthy and swore she had never suffered from the disease. Still, she was a danger to the public, so they shipped her off to an isolated cottage on North Brother Island in the East River. It was a tough break for Mary, but for the sake of the public, the Board of Health felt they needed to keep her in quarantine.

Eventually, she was set free after she promised never to work as a cook again. However, nearly five years later, in January 1915, typhoid broke out in the Sloane Maternity Hospital. Two people died and twenty-five people fell ill. And one of the healthy people was a cook named Mrs. Brown. It didn't take long to find out that Mrs. Brown was really Mary Mallon. This time around, there was no sympathy for Mary Mallon. She was sent back to the cottage and stayed there the rest of her life.

We at Weird Central have arguments about whether or not Typhoid Mary was a villain. Some of us think that she simply didn't understand how she could be healthy and still give people a disease. Others think that she should have counted her blessings when she was released and found another kind of work. Once or twice, we slap our foreheads and ask, "Why didn't she just wash her hands more often?" So what do you think? Was Typhoid Mary a villain or an unfortunate woman who meant no harm?

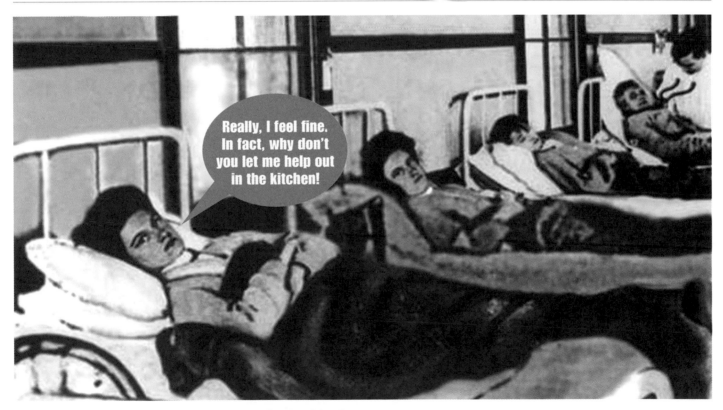

Mary Mallon at the quarantine hospital on North Brother Island.

Mrs. Cannon's Evil Trade

There's a library in Dover, Delaware, with a human skull in a closet, and that's not even the strange part. What is strange, however, is the story that goes with it. It's a story that dates back to the days of the Underground Railroad, and it involves kidnapping, slave trading, and murder.

Patty Cannon operated the most notorious crime ring in the Delmarva Peninsula in the early 1800s. This big, violent woman and her son-in-law used their taverns and boardinghouses as a front for all kinds of crimes, the worst of which was kidnapping free black people and selling them back into slavery. They held their victims in the basement or attic of their boardinghouses until they could sneak them out to slave traders.

Nobody's sure where Patty Cannon came from, but some say she was Canadian and married a Maryland man when she was quite young. They also say that soon after their daughter was born, Mrs. Cannon poisoned her husband and started building a criminal empire. She opened a tavern, where she cheated her clients and threatened them if they challenged her. They said she was so powerful she could throw a grown man to the ground by his hair. Her tavern attracted criminals who joined her gang, and for thirty years, they terrorized the area.

It all came to an end in 1829, when a local farmer plowed up a field near her property and found the bones of her gang's victims. The police arrested her, but she took poison and died before she could be convicted. She was buried in the jailhouse yard, and a hundred years later, her skull was uncovered by builders who were laying a new foundation. The skull was donated to the Dover Public Library, and that's where it's stored today. But don't worry: you can't borrow it!

This wig box contains the skull of Delaware's most notorious villain!

John Wilkes Booth

Soon after the Civil War ended, John Wilkes Booth went to Ford's Theatre in Washington, D.C., where the president was watching a play. He snuck up behind the president, shot him, and jumped onto the stage. He yelled, "*Sic semper tyrannis*"—a Latin phrase that means, "This always happens to tyrants"—and escaped into the night. Well, he sort of messed up the last bit, because he caught his foot as he leaped onstage, broke his leg, and had to hobble off. But that's only part of the story. The trouble with things that happened long ago is that you don't really know how it felt to people at the time. We know Lincoln was a hero, but we don't know much about the other guy, except that he was a killer. As with most things in life, there's a lot more to the story — most of it weird.

In fact, Lincoln wasn't loved by everyone in his own time. Many people didn't like his style of leadership, his style of dress, or even his hairstyle, for that matter. And weirdly enough, John Wilkes Booth was a pretty famous and popular guy. He was a good actor from a famous acting family. He had even been voted the handsomest man in America. Before he committed his famous crime, a lot of people liked him better than the president.

The Handsomest Assassin in America

John Wilkes Booth was born near Bel Air, Maryland, into a family of actors. His dad, Junius, was a famous Irish actor and his brother Edwin opened the famous Players Club in New York City—a place where actors can still hang out with other actors. Junius and Edwin are both celebrated with monuments and plaques in their hometown. If John Wilkes Booth hadn't done what he did, he'd probably have a statue in town, too. He was a very popular actor before the Civil War, and all the way through it.

Oddly enough, it was his career as an actor that got John Wilkes Booth involved in a plot against the president. During the Civil War, he was able to travel quite freely because of his job. He was from a state that was strictly speaking in the North but that had strong sympathies with the South, so the South approached John to join their spy network, the Confederate Secret Service. He transported information, met with many people in the service of the South, and got wind of a plot to kidnap President Lincoln. The idea was that they'd hold him hostage until the Union in the North released all their prisoners of war. John Wilkes Booth thought this was a pretty neat idea, but the Confederate president Jefferson Davis hated it, so the kidnap plot was dropped. Booth and his cronies still liked the idea, but when the war was over it made no sense to trade the president for prisoners of war. So they took it one step further and decided to kill him instead.

Handsome devil, aren't I?!

Escape

Right after the shooting, Booth escaped with his friend David Herold into Maryland. His first stop was a tavern in Clinton run by his friends the Surratt family, where he took guns to protect himself and whiskey to dull the pain of his broken leg. From there, he went to his friend Dr. Samuel Mudd's house in Bryantown for medical attention. And by the next morning, he was in Virginia.

What happened next seemed to surprise Booth. The reward for his capture went from $30,000 to $100,000 in a few days. He didn't understand this at all. He actually expected to be treated as a hero. That sounds strange, but here's what he wrote in his diary:

For striking down a greater tyrant than they ever knew, [I] am looked upon as a common cutthroat. I struck for my country and that alone. A country groaned beneath this tyranny and prayed for this end. Yet now behold the cold hand they extend to me . . . hunted like a dog through swamps, woods, and last night being chased by gun boats.

John Wilkes Booth may have been a good actor, but he didn't understand his audience. Within the week, the Union caught up with him as he hid in a shed near Port Royal, Virginia. He chose to die in a gun battle rather than be taken into custody.

Eventually, his body was buried in a private cemetery in Baltimore's Green Mount Cemetery. Nobody's sure where his body lies, but there is one unmarked grave in the plot owned by the Booth family, so people assume that's where he is. People often leave pennies on that grave—because the face on the head side of a penny belongs to the man he killed, Abraham Lincoln.

A Different Ending

There's another strange twist to this tale, however. Some people insist that Booth didn't die near Port Royal in April 1865. They say that the body that was found in Virginia and buried in Maryland was someone else's. The real Booth, they say, escaped to the West. The most famous tale is from a man named Finis Bates. Mr. Bates said that five years after the assassination, he met a man in Granbury, Texas, who called himself John St. Helen. He was a handsome man with a mustache and a very theatrical flair. He used to recite Shakespeare from memory. And when he felt that Finis Bates was his friend, he confessed that he was actually John Wilkes Booth. He told Bates that the night history said Booth died, he had lost his wallet and some papers and was out looking for them. His friend Ruddy had found them and was hiding in the barn when Union troops shot him. Because Ruddy was holding Booth's papers, everyone assumed he was Booth. That's what John St. Helen said, but Finis Bates thought his friend was kidding around.

Is the Booth mummy really history? Is it a mystery? Or is it a mad advertising scheme?

The two men fell out of touch with each other, but years later, Finis Bates heard that a man called David George had just confessed on his deathbed that he was really John Wilkes Booth. Mr. Bates went to see the body—and found his friend John St. Helen lying there in the morgue. He claimed the body of his old friend and had it made into a mummy. He used it as a sideshow exhibit, and the mummy of John Wilkes Booth was very popular from 1903 to the 1930s. It earned Mr. Bates up to $100,000 a year in admission fees—and that's more than five times what John Wilkes Booth earned every year as an actor.

But nobody's ever proved that the mummy was really John Wilkes Booth. The whole story of Booth's escape might just have been a clever way to get customers for Mr. Bates's mummy exhibit.

UNSUNG HEROES

f or every famous figure in America's past, there are hundreds of fascinating characters who never made the history books. For example, you might have read about Charles Lindbergh, the pilot who, in 1927, flew alone across the Atlantic Ocean without stopping and made aviation history. But you probably haven't heard of Douglas Corrigan, the first aviator to cross the Atlantic by mistake. Perhaps you're familiar with the famous wealthy recluse Howard Hughes. What about not-so-famous, not-so-wealthy recluses like New England's Leatherman and the Skunk Lady of Howe, Indiana? These individuals may never have done anything particularly important, but we still consider them heroes. Why? *Er* . . . well, we're easily impressed. Besides, in their own unique ways, these oddballs helped make America what it is today: weird!

All praise His Imperial Majesty Norton I!

America's First (and Only) Emperor

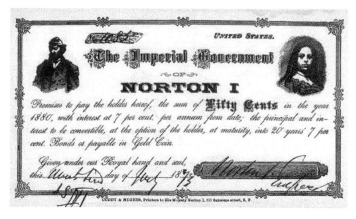

As everyone knows (or should know), America has never had an emperor. However, that didn't stop Joshua Abraham Norton (also known as His Imperial Majesty Norton I) from proclaiming himself Emperor of America.

Norton was born in England and moved to the San Francisco Bay Area in 1849. For a while, he thrived as a businessman by providing food and supplies to gold miners, but he lost his fortune and vanished from the Bay Area in 1858. Nine months later, he marched into the offices of the *San Francisco Bulletin* and asked them to print a statement that he had prepared. Oddly, the *Bulletin* followed his orders and printed it on the first page. (It must have been a slow news day in San Francisco.)

As self-declared Emperor of the United States and Protector of Mexico, Norton I proclaimed that it was unlawful for members of the U.S. Congress to meet. Ignoring him, they met anyway. Emperor Norton then instructed the army to arrest Congress. Naturally, they ignored his commands as well. Norton then set his sights a bit lower. He outlawed the word "Frisco," a shortened nickname for San Francisco.

Despite the fact that Norton was known to be a bit of a crackpot, many of the best restaurants in town offered him free meals

Funny money from the U.S.'s first and only emperor!

At the peremptory request and desire of a large majority of the citizens of these United States, I, Joshua Norton, formerly of Algoa Bay, Cape of Good Hope, and now for the last 9 years and 10 months past of San Francisco, California, declare and proclaim myself Emperor of these United States; and in virtue of the authority thereby in me vested, do hereby order and direct the representatives of the different states of the Union to assemble in Musical Hall, of this city, on the last day of February next, then and there to make such alterations in the existing laws of the Union as may ameliorate the evils under which the country is laboring, and thereby cause confidence to exist, both at home and abroad, in our stability and integrity.

Norton I

Emperor of the United States

February 16, 1859

and proudly displayed Imperial Certificates of Approval in their windows. Theaters reserved seats for him, policemen saluted when they saw him in the street, and newspapers printed his regal proclamations and wrote about his exploits. The citizens of San Francisco loved their unofficial emperor, so they made sure that he was never mistreated.

When Emperor Norton died in 1880, one newspaper announced his death with a headline he would have appreciated: LE ROI EST MORT ("The King Is Dead"). Residents gathered to mourn the loss of their local hero. Businessmen donated money to pay for a majestic rosewood casket, and as many as thirty thousand people showed up to march in his funeral procession.

Wrong Way Corrigan

It's one thing to make a wrong turn on the way to school, but it's something else entirely to fly a plane more than three thousand miles in the wrong direction. This achievement belongs to Douglas Corrigan, better known as "Wrong Way" Corrigan.

On May 20–21, 1927, Charles Lindbergh became the first pilot to fly solo and nonstop across the Atlantic Ocean, traveling from New York to Paris, France. Douglas Corrigan was one of the mechanics who helped build Lindbergh's plane. Corrigan was from Galveston, Texas, but he had Irish roots, and his dream was to follow in Lindbergh's footsteps—except he wanted to fly from New York to Dublin, Ireland. For two years, he tried to get permission for the flight, but authorities felt that an overseas trip would be too dangerous for Corrigan's rickety old airplane. Eventually, they let him attempt a route from California to New York and back again.

In 1938, he set out from Long Beach, California, and despite a leaky gas tank, he arrived in New York safely. Before the return trip, he refueled and added a few extra fuel tanks to his plane for good measure. According to his plan, the next step was to fly out over the

Atlantic and then make a U-turn and head back west. Instead, he flew east above the Atlantic Ocean and never turned around. Twenty-eight hours later, he landed in Dublin.

Hmm. You're probably wondering if Corrigan intentionally flew in the wrong direction so that he could make his dream come true. If so, Corrigan never admitted it. His story was simple: the fog was heavy, his compass wasn't working properly, and by the time he realized he had flown way off course, he didn't have enough gas to return to California.

This explanation might not sound entirely convincing, but it was good enough for the American public. The country was suffering through the Great Depression and times were tough. America was starved for a hero, so when the pilot returned, cheering fans threw him a ticker-tape parade. The headline of the *New York Post* read, HAIL TO WRONG WAY CORRIGAN, printed backward, of course.

Cordially Invited

In the late 1800s, Frank J. Wattron was the sheriff of a rough-and-tumble town called Holbrook in Navajo County, Arizona. Sure, Wattron was gritty and tough, but what we here at Weird Central like about him was his sense of humor. Sheriff Wattron's dry wit was best demonstrated by his handling of the case of George Smiley, a railroad worker who was sentenced to hang after killing his boss. No one had ever been executed in Holbrook before, so Sheriff Wattron wasn't exactly sure what to do. He was told that he needed to send out invitations. The sheriff joked with his men about how to word a card inviting folks to a hanging. Finally, he decided to mimic a wedding announcement.

The cards caused a scandal. President William McKinley even scolded the governor, and the governor postponed Smiley's execution so Wattron could come up with a more suitable invitation. This time he modeled it after a sympathy card. At the bottom of the card, he suggested that the governor form a committee to provide guidelines on how to write execution invitation cards. George Smiley was hanged on January 8, 1900. They say that he still haunts the Navajo County Courthouse. Employees insist that, at night, he slams doors and makes noises.

Holbrook, Arizona, *December 1* 1899.

Mr. *J. M. Pratt.*

You are hereby cordially invited to attend the hanging of one

George Smiley, Murderer.

His soul will be swung into eternity on December 8, 1899, at 2 o'clock p. m., sharp.

The latest improved methods in the art of scientific strangulation will be employed and everything possible will be done to make the surroundings cheerful and the execution a success.
F. J. WATTRON,
Sheriff of Navajo County.

Revised Statutes of Arizona. Penal Code, Title X., Sec. 1849, Page 807, makes it obligatory on Sheriff to issue invitations to executions, form (unfortunately) not prescribed.

Holbrook, Arizona, *1/7—* 1900.

Mr. *J. M. Pratt*

With feelings of profound sorrow and regret, I hereby invite you to attend and witness the private, decent and humane execution of a human being; name, George Smiley; crime, murder.

The said George Smiley will be executed on January 8, 1900, at 2 o'clock p. m.

You are expected to deport yourself in a respectful manner, and any "flippant" or "unseemly" language or conduct on your part will not be allowed. Conduct, on anyone's part, bordering on ribaldry and tending to mar the solemnity of the occasion will not be tolerated.
F. J. WATTRON,
Sheriff of Navajo County.

I would suggest that a committee, consisting of Governor Murphy, Editors Dunbar, Randolph and Hull, wait on our next legislature and have a form of invitation to executions embodied in our laws.

Sorry, I'm busy that day.

49

The Real Father of Our Country

We recently received an anonymous tip in the mail:

If you think that George Washington was the father of our country, YOU ARE WRONG!!!!!!!!!!!!!!!!
The REAL father of the UNITED STATES OF AMERICA was a man named JOHN HANSON!!!!!!!!!!!!!!!!! Ask Nick Pahys, Jr.
DDG-CH-AdVS-A.G.E.-LDA-FIBA, the founder of the One and Only Presidential Museum in the World.
HE'LL SET YOU STRAIGHT!!!!!!!!!!!!!!!!!

Of course, this letter made us curious. First of all, we'd never seen so many exclamation points in a note before, so we were sure that the writer was excited. And we wondered what all those letters were doing after Nick Pahys's name. Had the writer sneezed at the computer, accidentally typing random gobbledygook? These mysteries plagued us, but the most intriguing questions were: who was John Hanson, and was he truly the REAL father of our country?

John Hanson
Maryland
Our
1st President 1781

We discovered that there actually is a museum in Ohio called The One and Only Presidential Museum in the World. And the place is in fact run by a man named Nick Pahys, Jr. DDG-CH-AdVS-A.G.E.-LDA-FIBA. (The stream of letters wasn't a typo. What do they mean? Your guess is as good as ours.)

According to Nick Pahys, Jr., George Washington was not our first president. He was our ninth. Huh? It sounds ridiculous, but Nick explains that George Washington took office in 1789, after the U.S. Constitution was adopted in 1787. Before the Constitution, we had something called the Articles of Confederation. Pahys points out that eight presidents were elected under the Articles of Confederation, and each served a one-year term, including his hero . . . John Hanson. Hanson's accomplishments (according to Pahys) include creating the Seal of the President of the United States (an eagle bearing a shield, clutching arrows and an olive branch), declaring Thanksgiving a national holiday, and creating the U.S. Mint.

Check it out at www.oneandonlypresidentialmuseum.com.

Could all of this stuff be true? We did some research and soon had dates and names swimming in our heads. We learned that John Hanson was a very shadowy figure in American history. A lot has been written about him, but it's hard to separate the facts and the fiction. Besides, back before 1787, the country was somewhat disorganized. The U.S. Constitution set everything straight, and the first president under the Constitution was George Washington. So, who is the REAL father of our country? Our money is still on George Washington, but ultimately, this is another weird history question that will never be answered.

The First Nine Presidents of Weird U.S.

John Hanson
Elias Boudinot
Thomas Mifflin
Richard Henry Lee
John Hancock
Nathaniel Gorham
Arthur St. Clair
Cyrus Griffin
George Washington

Jim the Wonder Dog

Jim the Wonder Dog was no ordinary mutt. Many people who met him (and nuzzled his ears and scratched his belly, etc.) insist that he was the smartest dog in the history of dog-dom. Born in 1925, Jim didn't seem so special at first. He was one of many dogs in the Taylor kennels of Louisiana. Sam Van Arsdale, a hotelkeeper who lived in Marshall, Missouri, received the dog as a gift. It wasn't long before Mr. Van Arsdale realized that Jim was a very smart pup.

Dogs are thought to be red-green color-blind, which means that they can't tell the colors apart. But Jim had no problems with any colors. If he was asked to point out a man in a red tie or a girl in a blue dress, he would always answer correctly. Weirder still, Jim seemed to possess psychic powers. He could match owners to their cars. He could determine the sex of a baby before he or she was born. He could even predict the results of presidential elections and horse races. (He selected the winner of the Kentucky Derby seven years straight!) How did Jim communicate his Kentucky Derby picks? Van Arsdale wrote the names of the horses on pieces of paper and Jim put his paw on the winner's slip. Of course, this implies that Jim had another impressive talent. He could read! And being a worldly animal, he obeyed commands given in English, Spanish, Italian, French, and Greek.

Skeptics suspected that Van Arsdale was giving his dog signals. However, this doesn't explain how the dog could correctly answer questions that would have stumped his master, such as, "Who in this crowd has the most pocket change?" Throughout his lifetime, Jim turned doubters into believers. Veterinarians, university professors, and students were all flabbergasted by his incredible abilities.

On March 18, 1937, just after his twelfth birthday, Jim died of natural causes. Van Arsdale wanted to bury the dog in the Ridge Park Cemetery in Marshall, Missouri. This was against the rules, so Van Arsdale laid his pet to rest just outside the cemetery walls. Since then, Ridge Park has expanded to include Jim's grave. You can visit a statue of Jim inside the Jim the Wonder Dog Memorial Park.

Heroic Eccentrics

Everyone has their eccentricities, but some people are so jaw-droppingly weird that they become legends. We've read a lot about larger-than-life characters who seem to live in their own worlds with their own rules. One thing we've noticed is that, in most cases, these oddballs are not treated as outcasts. Instead, they're appreciated and often taken care of. Apparently, true weirdness brings out the best in people. Here are two bizarre and beloved examples.

The Skunk Lady of Howe, Indiana

"If you want to see the dirtiest woman in the world, go to Howe."

This piece of advice appeared on a poster that circulated around Elkhart, Indiana, in the early 1920s. Above the caption was a large photo of Christina Hahn D'Sullivan, better known as Crissy the Skunk Lady. According to an article in the LaGrange Standard in 1925, this poster caused quite a stir. Word spread and soon people were flocking to the town of Howe to catch a glimpse. Most ladies would be insulted to be called the dirtiest woman in the world, but not Crissy. In fact, when Crissy saw visitors approaching her tumbledown shack she would smear soot on herself because she wanted to look as filthy as possible.

Naturally, Crissy's poor hygiene made her rather smelly. Now, add a bunch of animals to the mix—dogs and cats, lizards and snakes, guinea pigs, chickens, and skunks. Keep adding more and more skunks, and you'll begin to imagine the intense odor that pervaded the D'Sullivan household. Crissy raised her skunks so that she could sell their fur, but often she grew attached and kept some as pets. The skunks shared her space and often slept on her bed. Anyone who could put up with her stinkiness could enjoy Crissy's company. She was even married a few times. But in her later years, she was a widow and her animals were her main source of companionship.

The residents of Howe, annoyed by the gawkers and the negative publicity, pitched in and bought Crissy a new house. Touched by their generosity, Crissy left her skunk companions and allowed her neighbors to give her a long-overdue bath. Then, a month or so after moving to her new home, she died. Tourists still visit Crissy the Skunk Woman's grave in LaGrange County and leave, of all things . . . flowers!

Come on in! Don't worry, I just took a bath . . . last year.

Pee-yew . . . what's that smell?

Leatherman

The story of Leatherman is simple, heartbreaking, and very weird. Jules Bourglay grew up in Lyons, France, in the 1820s. He came from a family of middle-class woodcutters, which became a problem when he fell in love with Margaret Laron, the daughter of a wealthy leather merchant. Margaret loved Jules but couldn't marry him because her father wouldn't give his consent due to Jules's background. They pleaded with Monsieur Laron until he proposed a compromise. He would let Jules work in his leather business. Then, after the boy learned the ropes, the lovers would be married.

All went well for a while. Jules worked hard and was promoted. Growing savvy in the world of business, he used his soon-to-be father-in-law's money to trade in leather and made a tidy profit. But Jules didn't see that new technologies would change the leather market, and he lost a fortune in 1855, ruining the company. He was too embarrassed to face Margaret and her father, so he disappeared.

Years later, in 1862, a man arrived in Connecticut with a strange outfit. He was covered from head to toe in a suit made of leather scraps stitched together. Looking a little like a beggar and a little like a leather-clad warrior, Jules Bourglay had come to America. He spent the next twenty-five years following the same path, trudging twelve miles a day in his leather suit. The outfit must have weighed more than sixty pounds, but it never slowed down Leatherman.

Leatherman modeling the latest in all-weather leather.

His 365-mile route, winding through parts of New York and Connecticut, took thirty-four days to complete, but he was always on schedule. Every thirty-four days, he would show up like clockwork. Why did he stick to his impossible schedule, wearing his unbearably heavy suit? No one knows. Aside from grunts and gestures, he never spoke or attempted to communicate with anyone, but once residents got used to him, they'd leave him food.

He lived in the wild, hunting and scavenging, and he slept in caves. He died in 1888 after suffering through a blizzard. Even more than a hundred years later, hikers seek out Leatherman's caves and trails, and some insist his ghost still walks the same 365-mile route.

One of Leatherman's caves.

ABANDONED PLACES

have you ever been left completely alone in your home? If so, did you suddenly think about how empty the place actually was, how quiet everything seemed to be? Did you listen for noises? Was it creepy? Now, can you imagine how much creepier it would be if, instead of standing in a regular house, you were standing in a whole empty town? Or on a steaming, empty piece of land that was once a town, but which rotted or fell apart years ago? Or how it would feel paddling down a river full of towering ships, every one of which is empty and rotting away to nothing? That's the kind of image that goes through our minds when we hear about abandoned places. And visiting places like these—or even just hearing about them—is about the creepiest feeling we can imagine.

Ghost Towns

We don't know about you, but whenever we hear the word "ghost town," we think of one of those black-and-white Western movies in which the hero rides his horse down an empty dirt street, past ramshackle wooden houses with broken windows, with tumbleweeds rolling past. But there's another kind of ghost town in the Weird world. It's the kind of place that's equally spooky but has a hint of something a little . . . well . . . strange about it.

The Hottest Ghost Town in America

The first thing you see is smoke rising from the ground. The next thing you notice is the smell—a mix of sulfur and burning rubber. And even on the coldest day of the year, the ground is warm—even hot. You're standing over an underground fire that has been burning for more than forty-five years and that could burn for another millennium. You are in Centralia.

This Pennsylvania town was once a bustling coal-mining community. But, just before Memorial Day in 1962, the town decided to burn some of its trash in the landfill, which was located in an old strip mine. The coal in the mine caught fire, and within a couple of weeks, foul, smelly flames were shooting out of the ground around town.

Instead of fixing the problem pronto, townsfolk spent a lot of time trying to avoid taking the blame. And so the fire continued. And though there have been attempts to extinguish the underground fire, things reached a head on Valentine's Day, 1981, when twelve-year-old Todd Domboski was nearly swallowed up by the ground. He was cutting through a yard when he found himself waist deep in the sinking earth. He screamed for help as he sank deeper into the ground and luckily, Todd's cousin saw the whole thing and dragged him out of the hole.

From that point on, people began leaving town. The noxious gases coming from the ground made people sick. The local gas station had to close down because the underground gas tanks were dangerously hot, and as people left, the government tore their houses down to ensure nobody else moved in. Even the road to Centralia collapsed.

A few houses still stand on Centralia's old South Street, and a handful of people still lived on the outskirts of the town when we last visited, but its streets are mostly empty of houses and uneven because the ground keeps caving in. It's an eerie sight to behold!

Lost Colony of Roanoke

The Outer Banks of North Carolina is the site of the first British colony in the New World—settled twenty years before Jamestown appeared in Virginia and more than thirty years before the Pilgrims landed at Plymouth Rock in Massachusetts. It's also one of the great mysteries in the history of the American colonies. That's because every single colonist disappeared with nary a trace, and to this day, no one knows what happened to them.

The colony was called Roanoke—not to be confused with the town of Roanoke in Virginia. (Actually, it's hard not to get confused, because in 1587 when this colony first appeared, North Carolina was part of Virginia.) One of Queen Elizabeth's favorite people, Sir Walter Raleigh, decided that England needed to establish itself in North America—mostly because they were jealous that the Spanish had already cornered the market on South America. So he sent a group of men to Roanoke Island in the Outer Banks, and a few years later sent 115 people to join them. Governor John White soon sailed back to England to ask for help in dealing with raids from neighboring tribes.

Why should Spain have all the fun?!

The Spanish Navy attacked England six months later, so Britain couldn't send any ships to visit the colony for two years. It was 1590 before White could return to the island. When he got there, the colony was gone. The houses and fortifications he had left two years earlier had been dismantled, and there was no sign of the more than one hundred colonists. As White's shipmates searched the island, they found three letters carved into a tree: CRO. A little further on, they found another carved word on a post: CROATAN. That was a good clue. The governor knew a friendly Native American named Manteo who lived nearby in a place called Croatan. If the settlers had been in any danger, they would have put a cross over the name; but there was no cross. Perhaps the colonists had just gone to live with Manteo and his tribe?

They tried to sail to the harbor on the mainland to find Manteo, but a storm blew up and sent them way off course, north into the Atlantic. By the time the weather blew over, they were already well on their way back to England. And by the time they got back, Walter Raleigh was out of favor with the Queen, and so nobody was interested in investigating what happened to the colony.

It was ten years later, when King James was on the English throne, before people from the colony at Jamestown began looking for traces of the Roanoke colony. Captain John Smith (of Pocahontas fame) turned up some clues, including a rumor that two white men, four boys, and a maid were working in a copper mine for an Indian tribe. And as for Croatan and Manteo's tribe, the last known point of contact with the Roanoke colony, well, nobody could track them down. Four hundred years later, we're still unsure of the Roanoke colony's fate.

WHITE'S PARTY FIND TRACES OF THE COLONISTS.

Perhaps all the colonists died shortly after John White left them. Perhaps they moved inland and settled somewhere else. Maybe they joined a local tribe of Indians and lived long and happy lives. We'll probably never know.

God's Own Ghost Town

Most major religions have one thing in common: they believe that God (by whatever name they call Him) created Earth. It's odd, then, that we at Weird Central could find only one place where God legally owned a piece of land. And it's even odder that it was taken from Him to pay off back taxes. God's own land was six square miles in the mountains of Sullivan County, Pennsylvania, and it used to be called Celestia. No buildings remain where Celestia once stood, because it has been abandoned since a few years after the Civil War. But it was once a thriving religious colony.

A Philadelphia paper merchant named Peter Armstrong bought some land in the mountains because of a Bible verse. Isaiah 2:2 says, "And it shall come to pass in the last days that the Lord's house shall be established in the top of the mountains." By Easter 1853, he had recruited hundreds of believers who began building homes there. Brother Armstrong didn't have a lot of money. To avoid paying taxes on

Peter Armstrong's grand vision.

All that's left of Celestia . . .

the land, which was in his name, he and his wife transferred ownership of the land to the "Creator and God of heaven and earth, and to His heirs in Jesus."

Once the land was legally God's country, Celestia thrived, but after a few years, the tax collectors came knocking. God, they said, may be the landowner, but His representatives at Celestia still owed taxes. Armstrong couldn't pay, so the county repossessed the land in 1876 and sold it at auction. The property went for $33.72, including $30.10 in back taxes. And the buyer was Peter Armstrong's son. But even though the property stayed in the Armstrong family, the city of Celestia gradually crumbled. You can still visit the streets of Celestia by driving along Route 42 from Laporte toward Eagles Mere. There's a historic marker at the right of the road, which is all that remains of God's own little place on Earth, which now belongs to the county's historical society.

Mary Celeste

On November 5, 1872, Captain Benjamin Briggs, an honest sailor, guided the *Mary Celeste* out of New York harbor and set off for Italy with a crew of seven experienced sailors, a large cargo, and two special guests—his wife and young daughter. This was before the days of satellite telephones and radios that could keep a ship in constant touch with the shore, so nobody was surprised when they didn't hear from the ship for a while. The big surprise came a month later, when the *Mary Celeste* was found drifting in the Mediterranean Sea, completely empty. One lifeboat was missing, but there was no sign that anybody had attacked the ship or that it had been in danger of sinking.

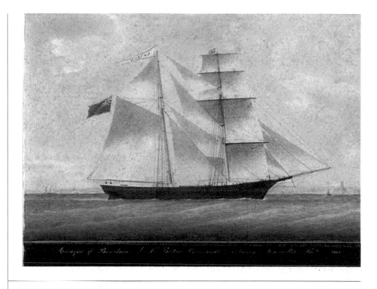

Benjamin Briggs, captain of the ill-fated *Mary Celeste*.

The crew of a British ship found the abandoned vessel and went aboard. They searched the captain's cabin and found his wife's jewelry and clothes untouched, his daughter's toys by the bed, and his logbook, with a final entry dated November 25 that made no mention of any trouble. The crew's quarters contained pipes and tobacco, with everything neatly stowed away, and the cargo was mostly intact. But a few important items were missing. The ship's navigator could not steer the ship properly without a sextant, chronometer, and book of maps. None of these were found. Also missing was the ship's register (basically, its ownership papers).

The mystery became an overnight sensation. Everyone wondered what had happened. Had they been attacked by pirates? Did they panic in a storm and abandon ship? Had there been a mutiny? Or was the captain in hiding, waiting to collect the insurance money on his ship? Everybody had a pet theory. Even the secretary of the U.S. Treasury went public with a lurid tale of the sailors murdering the captain in his sleep. We'll probably never know what happened to the crew of the *Mary Celeste*, and at this point, your guess is as good as anyone else's.

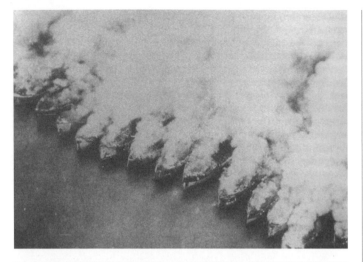

The Ghost Fleet of Mallows Bay

On April 2, 1917, President Woodrow Wilson brought the U.S. into the First World War. It had been raging for three years in Europe, and Imperial German submarines (they called them U-boats) had been destroying American ships. The U.S. Shipping Board Emergency Fleet Corporation was formed to produce ships for the war effort. Like many wartime projects, it was soon cranking out products fast—much faster, in fact, than the army needed them. When the war ended, the company had hundreds of wooden ships in stock, ordered and paid for, and essentially useless. Most of that fleet ended up at the end of the Potomac River at Mallows Bay, between Virginia and Maryland, and today, Mallows Bay is the largest ship graveyard in the U.S., possibly in the world.

The land around Mallows Bay came up for sale around the time that the ships needed to be scrapped, and so a salvage company bought it. They salvaged all the metal they could from the ships and towed the hulls out to the bay in the 1920s. There, they set fire to the wooden hulls. The original fleet was reduced to charcoal and ashes and ended up on the muddy bay bed. But from that day until now, Mallows Bay has been a refuge for stray ships. Whenever a ship around the Chesapeake needed to be scrapped, it ended up at Mallows Bay. At Sandy Point, on the north of the bay, stands a ship called *The Sentinel*, because it stands guard over the bay. That's not the ship's original name (nobody really knows that), but it's what boaters call it now. It was found floating in the river during World War II and was towed and tied up with steel cables to make sure it didn't drift away again. It's still there.

Mallows Bay is hard to get to unless you're part of an experienced kayak team, so you may never be able to see it in person. But if you're interested, there's a great history book about it called *Ghost Fleet of Mallows Bay* by Donald G. Shomette. Check it out.

Abandoned by the Army

War efforts like the ones that made Mallows Bay what it is today encourage companies to build quickly enough to win the war, but not always permanently enough to last. What happens when the U.S. Army withdraws from its old headquarters? They throw a perimeter fence around it, patrol it, and leave it to fall apart. In short, they treat it like these places you're now going to read about . . .

Fort Blunder: The Mistake on the Lake

Have you ever made a mistake that leaves you red-faced with embarrassment? If so, you'll have an idea of how the architect of Fort Montgomery felt way back in the early 1800s. Built on the shores of Lake Champlain in the northwest corner of New England, right where Vermont, New York, and Canada meet, Fort Montgomery is an imposing sight. After the British used this passageway to mount attacks against the U.S. during the Revolutionary War and the War of 1812, the U.S. said, "Enough is enough!" and built a huge fifty-cannon stone fortress, with all fifty cannons pointed north—where the British troops would come from if they ever dared to attack again.

Unfortunately, the British didn't need to fire a single shot to take Fort Montgomery. The American forces had built their fort a bit north of the border on Canadian land.

Fort Blunder has seen better days.

Fort Montgomery, ~~USA~~ . . . (oops) Canada.

And Canada was then under British rule. Oops! Instead of keeping the British out, the fort was a nice holiday home for them! Almost immediately, people began calling this stone castle "Fort Blunder," and snickering at the poor people who had lavished all the time and materials on building it. Fortunately, it was only under British rule for less than twenty years. In 1842, a treaty with Canada signed the land over to the U.S., and almost immediately, the U.S. Army began using the fort for training. For more than a hundred years now, it has been vacant, and locals have been taking stone from the walls for their own building projects ever since. The place is now an impressive ruin—best viewed from a safe distance away; since so many stones have been removed, it's now in danger of collapsing.

Nike Missile Bases

Before it became a brand of sneakers, Nike was best known as the name of the Greek goddess of victory. And back in the days of the Cold War in the 1950s and 1960s, the U.S. Army used that name for its missile defense program. The idea behind the Nike defense system was this: the army would set up a ring of bases all around Washington, D.C., with missiles that could knock out enemy missiles and aircraft before they could damage the center of government. The first bases appeared in Maryland and northern Virginia, but the idea was so popular that rings of Nike bases grew around big cities such as New York and Philadelphia, too. And they spread to California, Illinois, Ohio, and Texas.

Each Nike base contained radar towers, command and control centers, and underground bunkers filled with Ajax and Hercules missiles. And because they were designed to defend big cities, the bases were all built out in the suburbs, where lots of families lived. Everyone knew about them, but few people knew that some of these missiles had nuclear warheads. After the program was dismantled in the 1970s, many Nike sites fell into disrepair and decay, but a few of these sites have found new purposes. Some have become emergency management administration centers, and others were sold off and have been replaced by houses and offices. Some of the aboveground buildings now house retirement homes, community centers, and school district facilities. There is even one in Bucks County, north of Philadelphia, that is now the site of tennis courts.

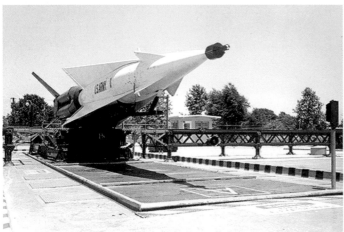

A Nike missile base in Pennsylvania before . . . and after.

Cape Henlopen

During World War II, the Army worried about German submarines and the damage they could do to ports and ships along the East Coast. So they set up defensive forts all along the Eastern Shore of Maryland and Delaware. As you drive the coastal road from Ocean City, Maryland, you can still see concrete platforms from which soldiers watched out for these subs. But for a real treat, you need to visit Cape Henlopen in Delaware. It's a state park now, but the U.S. Army ran a strategic defense post there until they gave it back to the State of Delaware in the 1960s. You can still see concrete watchtowers boarded up with plywood. There are concrete bunkers where they used to store huge guns. And if you can arrange a tour with a park ranger, you can actually walk around inside some of the buildings where soldiers used to watch out for sneak attacks. The only disappointment is that the guns have been removed. They were never fired during the war, anyway—Cape Henlopen captured only one U-boat during World War II, and it surrendered without a fight.

OLD-TIME ENTERTAINMENT

It's strange to see what people did for fun back before television, computers, cell phones, and video games. They'd go out to sideshows to see what we now watch on Animal Planet or the Discovery Channel—strange creatures; weird humans; and the largest, smallest, or oddest things that the entertainment business could turn up. They'd watch a woman lift up four grown men with a single finger. They'd go down to the biggest bridge in the state to watch a man dive off into the depths below. And when the entertainment really got weird, they'd pop a coin in a mummified murderer's mouth or rush out to shoot alien robots, convinced that the world was being taken over by creatures from Mars.

Don't get us wrong—we like Wii as much as anybody else, but doesn't that old-time entertainment sound like a pretty cool alternative?

If you've seen one bearded lady, you've seen them all.

A sideshow tent at the 1941 Rutland Fair in Vermont.

There's No Business Like Sideshow Business

You've probably been to a county fair or traveling circus or other type of fun carnival. These kinds of entertainment have been kicking around in the United States and Europe for hundreds of years. But you don't see one of the most important parts of the old-time fairground experience anymore: sideshows. You'd pay a dime to go into a maze of tents that contained strange animals and odd-looking people. In sideshows, the stranger the exhibit, the better. You'd see five-legged dogs, two-headed cows, incredibly tall and short humans, women with full beards, and more. Most of these exhibits were genuine oddities, but there were also several strange fakes including Zip, the What-Is-It?

What Is It?

Sideshow operators had a single mission: to talk up their exhibits so much that people just had to pay their dime to see what was hidden inside the show tent. The wild names they gave their exhibits were a testament to the power of advertising: who could resist Alphonso the Human Ostrich or Johnny the Half Boy? Well . . . after a while, people *could* resist attractions like these. After seeing one bearded lady, how much more exciting is it to see another? So the greatest sideshow operator of them all, P. T. Barnum, hit upon a new idea. Instead of telling people what was hidden inside the tent, why not just make them guess? That's how he came up with the idea of an exhibit called "What Is It?" Outside the tent hung the picture of a bizarre man-beast. Like many sideshow exhibits, the picture didn't really look like the guy inside the tent. In fact, it didn't take long before the question was answered. What Is It? Why, it's an English actor named Harvey Leech, that's what it is.

But Barnum wasn't about to let the fact that his first What-Is-It exhibit was known to be a fake get in the way. Soon, Leech was replaced by a genuinely strange-looking exhibit called Zip, the What-Is-It? This new model of What-Is-It had a long shaved head with a knot of hair at the top. He wore a gorilla suit. He made strange noises in his throat instead of speaking, but he was capable of playing tunes on a fiddle. He even wore a tux sometimes. Zip was billed as a survivor of a tribe from the Amazon, a missing link between humans and apes, and for years, that's exactly what people thought he was.

But in 1926, the year Zip died, his sister Sarah stepped forward and told a different story. Zip was really William H. Johnson, born in 1857 in Liberty Corners, New Jersey. He was one of six children and had been a circus performer long before Barnum cast him as his latest exhibit. Sarah said that William could "converse like the average person," and had "fair reasoning power." He had played the role of a strange creature for the money, and in six years, he had made a lot of it—$14,000—a small fortune in those days. He invested his earnings in a home and a chicken farm. And he had a great sense of humor about his strange job.

Though the Zip, What-Is-It exhibit played to racial stereotypes of the times, William Johnson had a sense of humor about his strange job. His dying words were, "Well, we fooled 'em for a long time." In the world of the sideshow, there's no greater memorial than that.

Really Close Twins

Every so often, you hear about twins who are actually connected to each other. They may be joined at the hip or chest, or even share a torso. Scientists call such people conjoined twins, but most people call them Siamese twins. That's because the most famous conjoined twins came from a country that was once called Siam. (It's now known as Thailand.)

Chang and Eng were born in 1811 in a small fishing village. They were joined at the chest by a bit of cartilage and a big blood vessel. Nowadays, surgeons can separate twins connected in this way, but that wasn't possible two hundred years ago. So they grew up together but acted pretty much like normal kids in the village—working in boats, fishing, and playing. But they attracted a lot of attention from visitors. Two of them, a sea captain named Abel Coffin and his passenger Robert Hunter, persuaded the boys to come away with them to perform in Europe. The teenagers did stunts to demonstrate their skills, played badminton against each other, and generally impressed the public. They eventually worked for P. T. Barnum, who advertised them as "Chang and Eng, the Amazing Siamese Twins."

The men worked for ten years in sideshows before buying a pig farm in 1839 in Wilkesboro, North Carolina. Four years later, they married a pair of sisters, Adelaide and Sara Yates. Nine months later, each couple had their first child—two daughters were born within six days of each other. Over the following thirty-five years, the two couples raised twenty-one children. But one day in 1874, Eng woke up to discover that his brother had died in the night. Chang had been sick with bronchitis, but his brother had not realized how sick he really was. Eng died shortly afterward.

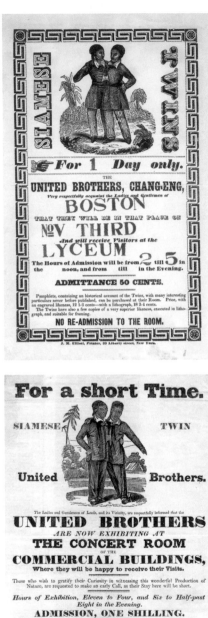

Posters advertising their shows called the twins "the United Brothers" and "a wonderful production of nature."

Two Hearts Beat as One

Strangely enough, Chang and Eng were not the only conjoined twins with connections to North Carolina. Mille-Christine McCoy was born there. We say "was," not "were," because Mille-Christine preferred to be thought of as a two-headed woman rather than twins. She had one spine and each head could feel sensations from the other body, and although she had two hearts, they beat at exactly the same rhythm. So she really was like a single person in many ways. But she had two heads and two different voices—a soprano and a contralto—so she could sing beautiful duets with herself. She worked at P. T. Barnum's circus as the Carolina Twin or the Two-Headed Nightingale until she was about fifty years old. Then she retired to North Carolina and lived the next twelve years with her large family of brothers and sisters. The two died within a few hours of each other on October 12, 1912, and are buried in a small family graveyard on the east side of Box High Road in Columbus County.

We are not a "we," we're a "she." See?

Although they were conjoined twins, Mille-Christine McCoy preferred to be thought of as one person.

The Georgia Wonder in action!

Lulu wrote in her autobiography that many of the early incidents at her home were pranks and her stage act was nothing supernatural but "manipulation of natural laws." Was she telling the truth or just trying to make people think she was a fake so she could live a normal life?

The Strange Strength of Lulu Hurst

Not all of the weird stage performers of the 1800s were strange looking. Lulu Hurst from Polk County, Georgia, looked like a perfectly normal young woman in her dark Victorian dress and neatly arranged hair. But she stopped looking normal quite quickly when her act got started. She would hold a billiard cue in one hand and offer it to a grown man in the audience. When he touched the end of the cue, he would be thrown around by some strange energy. She didn't exert herself at all, but the man who grabbed the cue would be huffing and puffing with the effort of staying upright. When Lulu touched a chair in her act—even with just one finger—nobody else could move it. And she could lift three men and the chair they were sitting in, all with one hand.

Lulu was observed by members of a medical college in Charleston, South Carolina, but nobody could figure out how she did it. She toured the U.S. for two years, causing great suspicion when she visited the Treasury in Washington, D.C. (officials were afraid she'd teleport the money out of the building) and tossed around a hundred members of the New York Athletic Club. Then she grew tired of being regarded as abnormal, and she retired. She went to college and eventually married her manager. To this day, nobody knows how she did her tricks or whether or not she possessed supernatural powers!

The World's Greatest Curiosity

Wherever Johnny Eck went, he left a lasting impression. He told wild tales, put on puppet shows for the kids in the neighborhood, and had many friends. Yes, you could say he was a large presence . . . even though he was less than two feet tall.

Johnny "Eck" Eckhardt was born in Baltimore, Maryland, in August 1911, a few minutes after his twin brother, Robert. And according to one of Johnny's classic yarns, the midwife screamed when she saw his useless, undeveloped legs, declared that he was "a broken doll," and fainted. Despite this inauspicious (and probably exaggerated) beginning, Johnny grew up secure and happy because of his supportive family. He learned to read and paint early in life, and was something of a celebrity at school, where his fellow students would fight over the privilege of carrying him up the stairs.

At a church magic show for poor and disabled children, a twelve-year-old Johnny impressed a stage conjuror named John McAslan when he walked

Aliens Invade New Jersey

In 1938, radio was the biggest form of entertainment in the U.S. People would cluster around big radio cabinets to listen to the latest tunes and radio plays. A smart young New York broadcaster named Orson Welles wanted to present a series of fake news bulletins. With Halloween approaching, he adapted a book about an alien invasion called *War of the Worlds* into a radio play. He made it all sound like a radio news report, and it was so realistic that people believed aliens had come in flying saucers from Mars to invade Earth.

Nobody was more scared by the broadcast than the residents of Grover's Mill, a tiny town in New Jersey, where the flying saucers were supposed to have landed. Early in the broadcast, Orson Welles pretended to be a news reporter doing a live broadcast from outside Grover's Mill. He announced that forty townsfolk and police officers lay dead there. The real townsfolk barricaded their doors, and some of the men grabbed shotguns and formed a posse to attack the alien invaders. Some of them were so scared they opened fire on a local man's water tower, thinking it was a giant robot Martian.

For years after, people in the town were embarrassed that they'd fallen for the hoax. But they weren't alone—smart city folk had been taken in, too. So on the fiftieth anniversary of the broadcast, the town erected a monument in Van Nest Park to celebrate the day that Grover's Mill defended Earth from alien invasion. On the radio, at least.

up to the stage on his hands. McAslan became Johnny's manager and toured him as "The Half Boy" and "The World's Greatest Living Curiosity." This was not just a freak show, though. Johnny was remarkably handsome and performed a skilled stage magic act on a tasseled stool, dressed in the top half of a tux. And photographs at the time show someone who really seemed to be enjoying himself. Johnny went on to appear in a few movies (including a stint in some Tarzan movies in the 1930s dressed up as a giant bird-like creature), and was cast (along with his brother) on a variety show called *Miracles*. In one classic skit, Robert Eck gets sawed in half, but of course, Robert switched places with Johnny and a dwarf engulfed in a large pair of pants. After sawing the box in half, the magician opened it, and Johnny chased his "lower half" around the stage.

Proof that the people of Grover's Mill are good sports

Alien invader or water tower?

PHOTOGRAPHED BY W. J. BOAG, PAWHUSKA, OKLA.

Got a nickel?

Mummy Entertainment

Just before the creepy, hokey boardwalk funhouse Laugh in the Dark in Long Beach, California, closed in 1976, it was used as a set in a popular TV show called *The Six Million Dollar Man*. The directors decided that a spooky old place with wax horror figures, ghosts, and fake skeletons would be a cool setting for an episode of the show. Little did they know they would find a real skeleton among the fakes and uncover one of the strangest forms of entertainment from the early 1900s.

The mystery began when a stagehand grabbed a wax dummy's left arm and broke it off. Underneath the wax, he found a real human bone. Medical examiners came in and removed the rest of the wax, uncovering a human mummy that had been killed by an old .32 caliber bullet. And inside the mummy's mouth were two strange clues: a penny dated 1924 and a ticket from the Museum of Crime in Los Angeles, California.

The ticket led investigators to identify the body as Elmer McCurdy—a career criminal who died in a shootout in 1911 after robbing a train in Oklahoma. The posse who shot him brought him to a nearby funeral home in Pawhuska. Nobody came to claim the body, so the undertaker came up with a novel idea to make some money. He pumped so much embalming fluid into old Elmer that he became a perfectly preserved mummy. The undertaker then invited people to come to his parlor and see "the bandit that wouldn't give up"—but only if they put a nickel in the mummy's mouth.

This bizarre exhibition carried on for five years, until two men asked for the body of their dear cousin Elmer. The undertaker couldn't refuse them, so he handed it over. But he had been tricked: the "cousins" were actually sideshow operators looking for another exhibit. They paraded Elmer throughout Texas with the same billing, "The Bandit that Wouldn't Give Up." He appeared in amusement parks, carnivals, in an open coffin in a wax museum, and even in a few movies. Nobody knows exactly how he came to Laugh in the Dark, but after the film crew found him, he finally got to rest in peace. He was shipped back to Guthrie, Oklahoma, given a proper funeral parade, and buried in Summit View Cemetery.

More Fun at the Funeral Parlor

Weirdly enough, Elmer McCurdy wasn't the only star in funeral parlor entertainment. People really did go to their local undertaker for fun back in the old days. Many states had laws that you had to embalm or bury a body a few days after he or she died. If nobody claimed the body, the funeral parlor that embalmed it would be responsible for it. They could store it or pay for it to be buried. Weird Central has received many letters from people who visited strange relics at the undertaker's. Here are just a few of them!

The next time you're bored with video games, head on over to the local funeral parlor!

Back in 1951 I heard of a mummy called "The Stone Man" in Lafayette, Indiana. At my stepfather's wake, I asked a young mortician who said, "Come to the fourth floor and see for yourself!" To my surprise, there it was: he was in an old coffin with a small window by his face. The story is that when he died, his family never claimed the body. First they moved him from room to room and then to the attic. Every time they sold the funeral home, the new owner got him along with the business. Little children used to be let in to see him in the 1940s for Halloween. They stopped it because he was too frightening to look at! —Richard Gray

When I was young, back in the early 1970s, everybody in my hometown of Shamokin, Pennsylvania, knew about the famous head at Farrow's Funeral Home on Sixth Street. It belonged to a murder victim they found in the mountains near Shamokin in 1904. They preserved it and put it on display so that somebody could identify who the victim was. Since the murder was never solved, the funeral home had to show the head to anybody who asked to see it. In 1976, they opened a museum celebrating the history of Shamokin, and they borrowed the head for an exhibit. A local judge didn't like what he saw and filed an injunction to force them to bury it. —ML

While working in a pharmacy in Middletown, Ohio, in 1982, I heard a clerk say that her parents had taken her to Urbana, Ohio, to see a "petrified man." I expressed disbelief but she insisted that the man was on display in a small shelter in downtown Urbana. She said his name was Eugene. Many years later, I told my uncle in Cincinnati that I had taken a fishing trip near Urbana, Ohio. He asked, "Is Eugene still there?" I was stunned. Could this be a true story? My uncle, then eighty-eight, said that he had seen this mummy on display, and he remembered a little of the story: a man who went only by the name Eugene had spent some time in Urbana. When he died, he was embalmed and placed on display in the town loop, with the hope that someone might come by and recognize him. My uncle did not know when he saw Eugene, but he thought it was in the mid 1950s. I still think this is a very weird story, but hearing it from two very diverse sources, I reluctantly believe it. —Tim Heenan

Sam Patch, the Jersey Jumper

Not all old-time entertainment was gruesome. Sometimes, it was just breathtaking and exciting. Take the mad stunts of Sam Patch, for example. When Sam was twenty years old and working in a cotton mill in Paterson, New Jersey, he announced that he was going to jump off the bridge over the Great Passaic Falls. Sure enough, on September 27, 1827, he stood on the new Chasm Bridge, praised the men who designed and built it, and threw himself over the edge of it. With his hands by his sides, he fell eighty feet to the deep water below and plunged below the surface. Tense moments passed, but Sam Patch returned to the surface and yelled a sentence that would become his slogan: "There's no mistake in Sam Patch!"

Newspapers and magazines across the country wrote about Sam's daring jump, and so he began to repeat the stunt—passing a hat around to earn a little money before leaping. When the crowds began to dwindle in Paterson, he went to Hoboken and jumped ninety feet off a ship's mast into the Hudson River. Then he began a jumping tour of the East Coast, leaping off anything high enough to look dangerous. He jumped off a giant ladder at Niagara Falls and survived a 130-foot drop—and did it a second time a week later.

But Sam's career as a daredevil jumper lasted only one year. After a successful leap off the Genesee Falls in Rochester, New York, he promised to repeat the stunt the next week—which happened to be Friday the Thirteenth, November 1829. That fateful day would be Sam's last jump. Witnesses saw him begin his trademark descent, arms by his sides and shooting down like an arrow. Then he went limp and his arms and legs thrashed about in the wind. He hit the water hard and disappeared. It took a search party two days to find him, and the doctor who examined him found that he had died before he hit the water.

The Great Falls area where Sam began his career hasn't changed much since his first jump. The Passaic still crashes beneath the same Chasm Bridge and runs past the mill where the Jersey Jumper once worked. And if you listen really carefully, somewhere in the crashing of the water, you may be able to hear an echo from the waterfall repeating a message from the past: "There's no mistake in Sam Patch."

The Great Falls of the Passaic River in Paterson, New Jersey, where Sam Patch jumped into the Weird history books.

Speaking of Great Falls . . .

Niagara Falls, straddling the U.S./Canada border, is a giant waterfall that drops 173 violent feet into the Niagara River. It's an awesome sight and a popular tourist destination. And back in the day, if you visited, you might have been able to catch a daredevil attempting to go over the falls in a barrel! More than a dozen people have purposely tossed themselves off the falls since Sam Patch first jumped off a platform at the top of a giant ladder into the Niagara River. Some of them lived; others . . . not so much. Annie Taylor (above left) was the first. She and her barrel went over the falls on October 24, 1901. She survived with only a scratch on her head,

although once out of the barrel, she said, "If it was with my dying breath I would caution anyone against attempting the feat. . . . I would sooner walk up to the mouth of a cannon, knowing it was going to blow me to pieces, than make another trip over the Falls." That, however, didn't stop Bobby Leach (above right) from becoming the second person to go over the falls on July 25, 1911. He survived but had to spend six months in the hospital recuperating from a broken jaw and two broken kneecaps.

IT'S WITCHCRAFT!

When settlers from Europe first came to this land, they left behind most of their possessions but they brought their superstitions from the Old World. And nothing frightened these early Americans more than the concept of witches and witchcraft. If crops failed or disease spread, they often assumed that it was the devil's handiwork.

Convinced that witches were among them, they launched desperate witch hunts, spreading terror and executing innocent people. These witch hunts are a sad, dark part of America's past, and fear of witches—or *wiccaphobia*—is one of the most common elements of our folklore. So if you're scared of witches, you're not alone. Wiccaphobia, it seems, is as American as Bigfoot hunting, UFO conspiracy theories, and apple pie.

There's nothing to be afraid of, dearie.

"Sarah Good came to me barefoot . . . and did most greviously torment me by pricking and pinching me and I veryly beleve that Sarah Good hath bewicked (bewitched) me." —Elizabeth Hubbard

The Salem Witch Trials

The *Mayflower* Pilgrims, who landed on Plymouth Rock in 1620, had come to the New World so they could practice their own religion—a form of Christianity called Puritanism. The success of their colony led to other settlements in New England. One such small settlement was Salem Village, Massachusetts, which today is called Danvers. The Puritans of New England were obsessed with purity and casting off their sins. They were ever watchful of themselves and their neighbors, and they were deeply frightened of witches and witchcraft. All of these factors came into play to bring about one of the darkest moments in American history.

It all started in January 1692 when Reverend Samuel Parris's nine-year-old daughter, Elizabeth, and his eleven-year-old niece, Abigail Williams, began acting strangely. They ran around screaming, throwing fits, and babbling nonsense. That may sound like normal playground behavior to you, but Samuel Parris didn't think so. And neither did the village doctor, William Griggs, who was convinced the girls were under the control of witches. Before long, three other girls began exhibiting weird behavior: Ann Putnam (eleven) and Mercy Lewis and Mary Walcott (both seventeen). They had seizures and went into trances. Was it epilepsy? Something they ate? Or were they just fooling around?

Ultimately, the Reverend Parris decided to use "spectral evidence" to reveal the identities of the witches. The theory behind spectral evidence was simple: if you're a victim of witchcraft, then you can see things that no one else can see. For example, sometimes in the dark, you might glimpse the ghostly image of the witch responsible for enchanting you. The adults gathered the children together and asked if they saw apparitions at night. The girls mentioned a slave woman named Tituba and insisted that she was a witch. After all, Tituba was from Barbados and may have told them stories of voodoo and folk magic.

The Reverend George Burroughs was accused and convicted of being "the ringleader of them all."

The Witch House is the only building still standing in Salem with direct ties to the witch trials. It was the home of Judge Jonathan Corwin, who served on the court that sent nineteen people to their deaths. It's now a museum.

They also picked a beggar named Sarah Good and a reclusive old woman, Sarah Osborne. (Like Tituba, these poor outcasts must have looked like witches to the imaginative girls.) Sarah Good and Sarah Osborne pled innocent, but Tituba confessed to practicing witchcraft. She testified that she knew of other witches in Salem Village and confirmed that Sarah Good and Sarah Osborne were part of the satanic conspiracy. Why did Tituba make these statements? We can't be sure, but, most likely, she was told that a confession would save her life, so like many others, she made one up.

> "I am wronged. It is a shameful thing that you should mind these folks that are out of their wits."
> —Martha Carrier (hanged on August 19, 1692)

News of Tituba's testimony spread quickly, and the townspeople began to panic, imagining apparitions and making accusations. Hearings were held, and they were often wild affairs. One of the accused was an elderly woman, Rebecca Nurse, who was respected and deeply religious. Abigail Williams and Ann Putnam insisted that they had seen the old woman's specter, and they were present at the trial, eager to see Rebecca Nurse convicted. Supposedly, after the jury found the defendant not guilty, the children contorted their faces and twisted about, making believe that the old woman was attacking them. The chief justice then had the jury reconsider their decision. In the end, Rebecca Nurse was declared guilty. To the girls, the trials were just a game. In fact, later on, one of the children said, "We must have our sport."

"Oh, Lord, help me! It is false. I am clear. For my life now lies in your hands."
—Rebecca Nurse
(hanged July 19, 1692)

The Salem Witch Trials Memorial.

In May 1693, more than 150 people had been accused of practicing witchcraft in and around Salem Village. Fourteen innocent women and five innocent men had been hanged. Another man, Giles Corey, had been crushed to death under a board covered with heavy rocks. Magistrates performed this form of torture, called "pressing," to extract a confession. Eventually, the panic died down and the town regretted its actions. Sir William Phips, the colonial governor of Massachusetts, declared that spectral evidence could no longer be used in a court of law. In 1702, the trials were declared unlawful. Ann Putnam, one of the accusers, publicly apologized for her actions in 1706, and Massachusetts formally apologized for the witch trials . . . in 1957.

Salem has come to terms with its past and is now a tourist attraction.

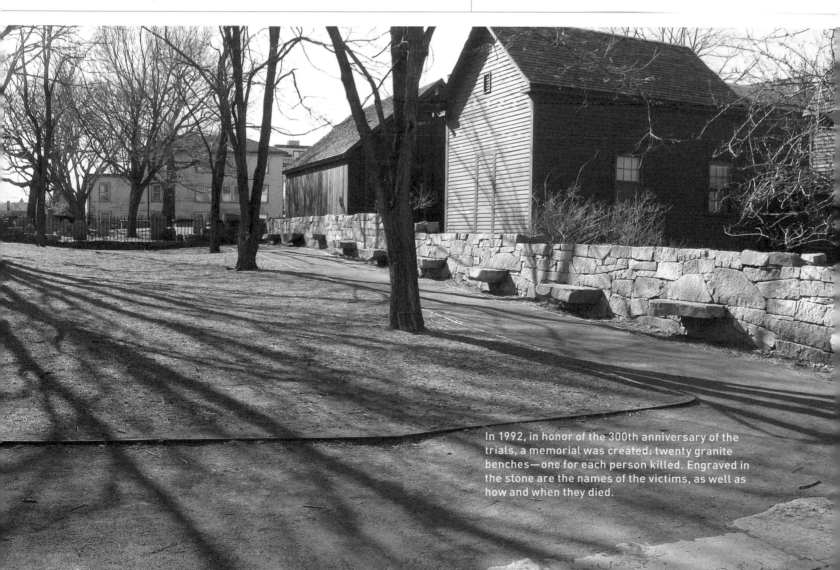

In 1992, in honor of the 300th anniversary of the trials, a memorial was created: twenty granite benches—one for each person killed. Engraved in the stone are the names of the victims, as well as how and when they died.

The Witch of Ridley Creek

A few years before the hysteria in Salem Village, a small witch hunt took place near Philadelphia, Pennsylvania. Fortunately, William Penn, the founder of Pennsylvania—and a man known for his honesty and fairness—was around to keep things under control.

The witch trial was held in January 1684. Farmers had been suspicious of their neighbor Margaret Mattson for years, mostly because she had the biggest farm around and they were envious. Also, she sounded very strange to her neighbors—she was Swedish and spoke very little English. They called her the Witch of Ridley Creek so often that eventually she was formally charged with witchcraft.

Grab her! She bewitched my cows!

William Penn conducted the hearing, and the accusations were so vague that Penn was convinced of only one thing: Mrs. Mattson's neighbors didn't like her. One man swore that someone told him Margaret Mattson had bewitched several cows. Another witness claimed that his friend's wife had been threatened by an apparition sent to her by Mrs. Mattson. Penn dismissed all these rumors, but then he asked her a question that caused a sensation. Expecting the answer "no," he turned to the accused and asked: "Art thou a witch? Hast thou ridden through the air on a broomstick?" Possibly because of language difficulties, the woman answered, "Yes."

This put Penn in an awkward position. The Witch of Ridley Creek had essentially confessed to a serious crime, so Penn had to think fast to keep her alive. According to local legends and a few history books, Penn said that there was no law against riding on broomsticks, and he recommended she be set free. Because she had actually admitted to being a witch in court, she could not be let off entirely, so the verdict was that Margaret Mattson was guilty of being called a witch but not guilty of *being* one. Mrs. Mattson was released on bail and never came into the court again.

Um . . . there's no law against riding around on a broomstick.

The Mount Holly Witch Trials

On October 22, 1730, an article in the *Pennsylvania Gazette* described a witch trial at Mount Holly, New Jersey. The details of the case were astounding: a man and a woman were being tried for bewitching farm animals. According to the *Gazette*, "The accused had been charged with making their neighbors' sheep dance in an uncommon manner, and with causing hogs to speak and sing psalms."

The piece goes on to describe a series of "experiments" that were performed in order to prove that the alleged witch and warlock were guilty. But to assure fairness, the man and woman insisted that some accusers be put to the same tests. So, before three hundred witnesses, the accused and the accusers were weighed on a scale against the Bible. It was believed that the witches would weigh less than the Holy Book, but everyone who was put on the scale was heavier. Next was the trial by water. The accused and the accusers had their hands tied and they were dunked underwater. It was believed that anyone guilty of witchcraft would float. The innocent would sink. Spellbound, the crowd watched and gasped when they saw the two defendants floating on the surface of the water. But something was wrong: one of the accusers was floating as well. Panicking, she insisted that she be dunked repeatedly until the devil was dunked out of her. In the end, the results were unclear and the trials were postponed until the weather was warmer.

Many historians believe that the article was a hoax written by the owner of the *Pennsylvania Gazette*, a young upstart named Benjamin Franklin. Why would Benjamin Franklin make up a story about sheep dancing and pigs singing gospel songs? Was he just goofing around, or was he making fun of the Mount Holly residents for being backward and superstitious? It's hard to know with Benjamin Franklin.

So wait, let me see if I've got this right: if she floats she's a witch, and if she sinks, she's not . . . but then she's drowned!

Moll Dyer's handprint.

The Legend of Moll Dyer

In Leonardtown, Maryland, there's an 875-pound boulder called Moll Dyer Rock. There's also a road called Moll Dyer Road and a stream called Moll Dyer Stream. There are songs about Moll Dyer, and even a ballet based on Moll Dyer's life. Who is Moll Dyer and why is everyone so interested in her? Some folks in Leonardtown will swear that she was a witch. Some will say that she was an innocent woman who was persecuted by an ignorant mob of witch hunters. And others will scoff and insist that she never even existed.

There are many different legends about Moll Dyer. In one version of the story, she was an ugly old witch who lived deep in the forest. Bitter and lonely, she cast spells on the townspeople of Leonardtown, spreading disease and misfortune, and making children run wild, barking like dogs. Other Moll Dyer legends are more flattering. These tales paint a picture of Moll Dyer as an herbalist—a woman who lived in the woods and created natural cures for the residents of Leonardtown. But all stories about Moll Dyer agree about one thing . . . sometime around 1697, the townspeople turned against her. Convinced she was a witch, they blamed their hardships on Moll Dyer and decided to hunt her down and kill her. The mob burned down her house, but Moll Dyer escaped the fire. She raced into the forest, but she didn't get far. The woods were too dark and the weather was brutally cold. Days later, her body was discovered, frozen solid against a large rock. The villagers were able to chip her free, but they were never able to erase the mark of Moll Dyer. To this day, the boulder bears her handprint.

You can visit Moll Dyer's Rock outside the St. Mary's Historical Society in Leonardtown. But this is one tourist attraction with a dark side. Many visitors claim that a gloomy presence hangs over Leonardtown. They say that the town is cursed by Moll Dyer's ghost and that touching her rock can make you sick. If you wander through the woods at night, you might catch a glimpse of the ghost. Locals have spotted her running along Moll Dyer Road, still trying to escape her pursuers more than three hundred years after her death.

Witchcraft and Murder in Hex Hollow

Hex Hollow, also known as Spring Valley Park and Rehmeyer's Hollow, is in southern York County in Pennsylvania. It's a maze of trails and dirt roads twisting in and out of each other. There's a lonely grave in Hex Hollow where Nelson Rehmeyer, a black magician, is buried.

Most of the area is a county park now, but it's not well used, partly because it's off the beaten track but mostly because it's Hex Hollow. It's not easy to find, but you know it when you're there. The world becomes a little darker. How much darker it must have been in 1928, when the hollow's one resident was Nelson D. Rehmeyer—a loner well over six feet tall, with deep-set eyes and a powerful presence. Rehmeyer was what is commonly called in this area a powwow doctor. They are also called Brauchers or, in a more negative light, Hexenmeisters, or just Hexers. In Rehmeyer's time, there were hundreds of informal powwow practitioners throughout this area. One was named John Blymire, a sickly and sad man from a family of Brauchers who traced their spiritual lineage back to Pennsylvania's most famous witch, Mountain Mary. But John Blymire could keep none of his powwow patients. He could figure out no explanation for his hardship, save perhaps the answer obvious to someone of his background: he must have been hexed. He soon figured that Rehmeyer was the one who cursed him.

Blymire knew that in order to break the curse, he needed Rehmeyer's hex book. He quickly enlisted two teenage boys to confront Rehmeyer. They wrestled the powerful Rehmeyer to the ground, but when he failed to give up the book, they killed him. Now, most people don't know the real story of the place, but they know to stay away, especially at night.

After killing Rehmeyer, Blymire and his cohorts were too spooked to search the house for the hex book.

Witches Holidays Explained

Recently, we received an angry letter from a witch. The writer complained that, by sharing folktales about witches, we were spreading wiccaphobia. We decided to do some research and learned a lot about witches who practice a modern form of witchcraft called Wicca. For example, we discovered that most modern witches celebrate holidays that were originally created by ancient nature worshippers, or pagans. As you read about these pagan holidays, you'll probably notice that they sound very familiar. This is no coincidence.

Early Christians created holidays that overlapped with pagan ones, hoping their celebrations would eclipse them. Instead something strange happened: the two sets of holidays intermingled. That's why certain Christian holidays are full of pagan traditions. So, to help rid the world of wiccaphobia, we now bring you some interesting history about pagan holidays. And, to whoever wrote the letter: please don't put a hex on us!

The Festival of the Trees

Cultures that worshipped nature paid special attention to moments when the seasons changed. These moments are called equinoxes and solstices, and so the four biggest pagan holidays are the winter and summer solstices and the spring and fall equinoxes.

The Festival of the Trees, also known as Ostara, is a celebration of the spring equinox and comes on the first day of spring, between March 20 and March 22. Important symbols during the festival are rabbits (representing fertility) and eggs (representing birth). More than 2,500 years ago, to celebrate the spring equinox the ancient Persians would often decorate eggs. Painted eggs? Bunnies? It's obvious by now that Easter is an example of a modern religious holiday with a lot of ancient pagan trimmings. Even the name, Easter, has pagan origins. It comes from the Saxons of Northern Europe. Their goddess of fertility was called Eostre.

Ostara was an egg-celent holiday!

Yuletide

As winter dragged on and days grew shorter and shorter, some high-strung pagans worried that the sun was going away for good. That's why they viewed the winter solstice or Yuletide as the birthday of the sun—the time of year to breathe a sigh of relief and say, "Finally! The days are going to get longer again!" To the pagans it was about rejuvenation, and to symbolize the holiday they decorated evergreen trees, because they stayed green all year round. This tradition lives on today every time someone puts an ornament on a Christmas tree. And, sure enough, the annual winter solstice comes on the shortest day of the year, between December 20 and December 23, right around Christmas.

Centuries ago, in Ireland and England, jack-o'-lanterns were carved out of turnips and large beets to scare away evil spirits. Immigrants from these countries came to the U.S. and found that the native pumpkins were great for carving scary faces!

Samhain

Okay . . . we've mentioned Christmas and Easter. What other holiday do you think has elements left over from pre-Christian, pagan times? Of course, the answer is Halloween. Long before it became known as Halloween, there was a festival in late October called Samhain, which means "Summer's end." Samhain marked the end of the harvest for the old Irish, or Celtic, people. It was a time of bonfires and sacrifices, a weird night when the dead were allowed to return to Earth. To ward off evil spirits, it made sense to the ancient Celts to keep costumes and masks close at hand. So how did Samhain become Halloween? Around the year 610, Pope Boniface IV decided to move All Saints' Day from May 13 to November 1. All Saints' Day is also known as All Hallows' Day, which makes October 31 All Hallows' Eve, or Halloween, for short.

Walpurgis Night

Halloween can get pretty spooky, but the creepiest festival on the pagan calendar is on April 30, a holiday called Walpurgis Night. In Germany, Walpurgis Night (or Walpurgisnacht) is also known as Hexennacht, the Night of the Witches. They say that, on Hexennacht, witches from all around the world gather together. Some ride on broomsticks. Others ride on goats. And they meet on top of the Brocken, the highest peak of the Harz Mountains in Northern Germany. This fabled event has turned the Harz region into a tourist destination for real-life witches.

SECRET SOCIETIES

most of us belong to some kind of club or group. It might be the chess club or drama team at school or a group of kids who like to play a certain sport after school. It might even be the kids in the lunchroom who share secrets with each other but who clam up quickly when anybody else comes around.

There are a few strange societies in America's history that are just as secretive as those kids in the lunchroom, but some people feel that these groups are up to no good. These groups meet secretly, perform strange rituals, and tell nobody about what they do. They're definitely a part of U.S. history, but just how much so is anyone's guess!

George Washington is the U.S.'s most famous Mason, and many historians say that when Washington raised large armies to fight the War of Independence, many of those fighters were Masons.

The Freemasons

Few groups have as many conspiracy theories attached to them as the Freemasons (often just called Masons). This group was started by stoneworkers in the early 1700s, and today it has up to six million members around the world. You've probably gone past a place in your hometown with a Masonic Lodge sign outside it. Most people think of the Masons as a kind of club—a fraternal organization. But then why do they have secret rituals with mysterious handshakes? Why do they wear leather aprons with odd symbols on them? What are they trying to hide?

Whatever the answers to these questions might be, one thing's for sure: the Masons have been in the U.S. since long before it was the United States. The first Masons were a union of builders in Europe, and many of them came to the New World. In fact, as a group, they believed in the kind of ideas that America was built on, including religious tolerance and the proposition that all men are created equal. These radical beliefs made kings and other leaders in Europe very suspicious of the Masons—it was ideas like this that led to revolutions. So, rumors were spread that the Masons were sinister and up to no good. This, along with the facts that many influential American leaders have been Masons and that members don't talk much about what they do, has led to many theories as to what goes on behind the closed doors of Masonic lodges.

According to some people, Masons have been involved in the assassinations of both Abraham Lincoln and John F. Kennedy, financial catastrophes, the staged (fake!) moon landing, the sinking of the *Titanic*, and the secret running of the whole entire world. Sometimes it feels like if it rains on a parade, someone will blame the Masons! As far as we can tell, the Masons didn't have anything to do with these events, and if they are secretly running the world, they're not doing a very good job!

Masonic symbols such as this one appear on many buildings in and around Washington, D.C., and around the world

The Masonic National Memorial, just outside our nation's capital in Alexandria, Virginia. Some people think it's the secret meeting place of the mysterious people who really run this country.

The City the Masons Built?

Some people say the city of Washington, D.C., is one large Masonic symbol. For one thing, the architect of the city, Pierre Charles L'Enfant, was a Freemason. And how else can you explain this: the classic Masonic image (a compass and a straight edge) can be traced on the map of D.C. Look at the satellite image of the city on the right, and connect the Capitol (1) to the White House (2) and the Jefferson Memorial (3) to form the compass. Then join the Capitol (1) to the Washington Monument (4), and draw a straight line from the Washington Monument to the House of the Temple (5) (a Masonic temple in D.C.) and presto! You have a Masonic straight edge.

It's clear that Washington was not designed for easy driving or tourism—all the squares, circles, and dead-end roads are enough to disorient any visitor. But perhaps the city planners' original intention was not ease of navigation but to honor a mysterious secret society instead.

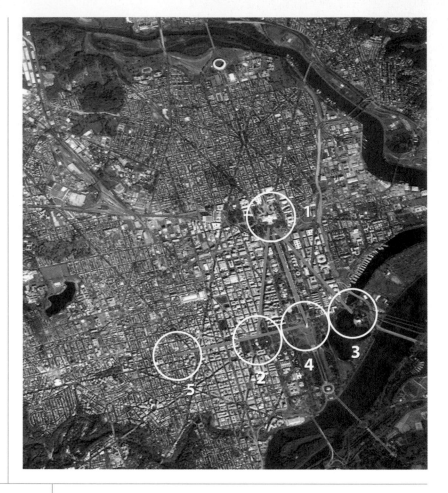

Aliens Rule Washington

At 16th Street and S Street in Washington, D.C., stands the House of the Temple, the headquarters of the Scottish Rite of Freemasonry. If the legends are true, beneath it lies a warren of tunnels inhabited by aliens. Supposedly, the tunnels were built eons ago by a race of people known as Atlanteans. These tunnels lead to a massive cave known as Nod, where the National Security Agency meets up with a number of alien races, among them a group of beings known as the Sirians.

Welcome to the House of the Temple. Aliens, please use the side door.

Is Buzz Aldrin on the moon or in some
Freemason's basement?

The Woman in the Wilderness

On a ridge above Philadelphia's Wissahickon Creek, right in the middle of Fairmount Park, there's a gravel road through the woods called Forbidden Drive. It's not far from Hermit Lane, Hermit Street, and Hermit Terrace. So, you're probably wondering . . . who's the hermit? Well, his name was Johannes Kelpius, and he was the leader of a secret society of brilliant men from Transylvania who moved just outside Philadelphia in 1694. These so-called monks composed music for the churches down in the valley and practiced medicine. Legend has it they also practiced magic and believed the end of the world was coming . . . soon. They looked to the skies for signs and they even started referring to themselves as The Woman in the Wilderness—a strange name for a group of men, but they were referring to a verse in the last book of the Bible, Revelation, which described the last days of the world.

People in the city below started to wonder about the group. Some said that the monks went into trances and could see things from many miles away. One story told of a woman who went to the monks because she didn't know when her sailor husband would return. A monk went into a trance and said her husband was in London, England, and would be returning soon. A few weeks later, the husband arrived with a story that a monk had come up to him in London and told him to return home. The monk in the trance had left his body and materialized three thousand miles away!

You can still visit the Cave of Kelpius on the ridge above Wissahickon Creek. It's not signposted, but if you clamber up the hillside, you'll find it tucked away next to a massive stone marker that says Kelpius belonged to the first Rosicrucian colony in America.

The Mystic Order of the Rosicrucians

The Rosicrucians are an ancient order of mystics originating in Europe. They found their way to America in the early twentieth century as a mail-order business selling "spiritual illumination" (whatever that is!). The group called AMORC (the Ancient Mystical Order Rosae Crucis) first came to the public's attention in 1915, when a businessman named Harvey Spencer Lewis made a grand announcement: the pharaoh Akhenaton's secret society was now taking applications.

As its imperator (or leader), Lewis claimed that his group began in ancient Egypt and worked its way through 108-year cycles of public and private activity, with many great men in history as members. Other Rosicrucian groups disputed this, but Lewis gained popularity and AMORC thrived. Their ads still appear in countless magazines, promising the secrets of "cosmic consciousness" to sincere seekers.

And even if you feel slightly suspicious about this secret society, you should definitely check out its headquarters in San Jose, California, which is a block-sized park that includes sphinxes, pyramids, planetariums, elaborate fountains, grand temples, and a museum that houses the largest collection of ancient Egyptian relics on the West Coast. Also here is the secretive Supreme Temple. What goes on in there? Don't ask us—find a Rosicrucian and let us know what you find out!

Inside the Rosicrucian Egyptian Museum.

Skull and Bones

Pirates aren't the only group of people who use a skull and bones as their symbol. There's a group that's been going for nearly two hundred years that also loves the skull and bones. In fact, it loves them so much, that's what it's called.

Don't ask how the Skull and Bones society got its name. Don't ask why its windowless headquarters on High Street in New Haven, Connecticut, is called the Tomb. You really don't want to know that this Yale University fraternity really does contain skulls and bones. You don't want to know that since it first started in 1832, the Skull and Bones society has produced many people who ended up ruling this country and leading its industrial and financial companies. (Hmm . . . conspiracy, anyone?) You can live without knowing that George W. Bush, his father, George H. W. Bush, and his grandfather, Prescott Bush, were all Skull and Bones men.

In fact, Grandpa Bush was behind one of the more enduring legends of the Skull and Bones society. They say that Prescott Bush dug up the bones of Geronimo, nine years after the great Apache warrior died at Fort Sill, Oklahoma. Who knows whether or not this story is true? We don't, but we do know that some Skull and Bones men proudly boast that it's true and that a man who used to be a member of the group reported the story to an agency of the federal government that investigated it. Other grisly trophies are said to be secreted away within: Hitler's personal silverware, the founder of Yale's gravestone, and even a third prized skull, one that once belonged to the Mexican hero Pancho Villa.

Our research found out one solid fact about the Skull and Bones society that may or may not be relevant. Apparently, the building they call the Tomb, where the Skull and Bones men meet, has the highest water bill in all of New Haven. If you want to solve a mystery, don't think about how to prove they stole Geronimo's skull. Think about what they could be doing with all that water. That may be the weirdest thing of all.

Mysteries of the Dollar Bill

Symbols are pictures that mean something special to people. You take one look at a symbol and you know immediately what it means. The glowing outline of a green person at a crosswalk is a symbol meaning that you can walk. An outline of a person wearing a skirt on a door in a restaurant means the door leads to a ladies' restroom. These are all symbols everyone understands. The trouble is that some symbols aren't so obvious. And when we looked closely at a U.S. dollar bill, we found symbols that confused us. It's not surprising, really. Brilliant men such as Thomas Jefferson and Benjamin Franklin had a hand in designing bits of the dollar bill, and they were deeply into codes and symbols. Jefferson even designed a code that kept secrets from the British during the War of Independence. So you can imagine they wouldn't think of simple things to put in their designs. Now, we've spent our fair share of dollars, but we'd never really taken our time to look closely at the bill itself. When we did, we started to wonder what in the world we were looking at.

The Pyramid, the Eye, and the Freemasons

If you turn over the bill, you'll see two circles. These are the two sides of the Great Seal of the United States. The First Continental Congress requested that Benjamin Franklin and a group of men come up with a seal. It took them four years to accomplish this task and another two years to get it approved. If you look at the left-hand circle, you'll see a pyramid with the top missing.

For many people, the dollar bill is full of clues that the U.S. was part of a conspiracy by the Freemasons to take over the world. The signs are there for all to see. The biggest Masonic symbol on the dollar bill is the portrait of George Washington, who was a member of

Facts about the Dollar Bill

- This so-called paper money is in fact a cotton and linen blend, with tiny red and blue silk fibers running through it. (It won't fall apart in the washing machine.)
- A special, secret blend of ink is used.
- Each bill is overprinted with symbols, and then it's starched to make it water resistant and pressed to give it that nice crisp look.

two different Masonic lodges. The unfinished pyramid showing two sides of thirteen layers is entirely Masonic—the original Masons were all builders and architects. At the top of the pyramid inside a triangle is the all-seeing eye—a well-known Masonic symbol for God. The motto *"annuit coeptis"* near the eye means "he has favored our undertaking." To the Masons, that would mean that God supports their plan to take over the world.

Meanwhile, if you look on the front of the dollar bill, you'll see the U.S. Treasury Seal. In the center you have a carpenter's set square, a tool used for measuring an even

cut. It's also a symbol that the Masons have used for centuries. Some people believe that it's proof that the Masons have taken over the banking system as part of their plan to rule the world.

So, how much of this is true? Luckily for us, Charles Thomson, the man who submitted the final design of the Great Seal, actually described what the symbols in the Great Seal meant when he presented the design to Congress.

Here is Charles Thomson's explanation of the symbols:

• The stripes (on the shield) represent the several states all joined in one . . . supporting a chief which unites the whole, and represents Congress.

• The motto (*E pluribus unum*—one made out of many) alludes to this union.

• The stripes in the arms are kept closely united by the chief and the chief depends upon that union . . . to denote the Confederacy of the United States and the preservation of their union through Congress.

• The olive branch and arrows denote the power of peace and war, which is exclusively vested in Congress.

- The stars denote a new state taking its place and rank among other sovereign powers.

- The shield is borne on the breast of an American eagle without any other supporters, to denote that the United States of America ought to rely on its own virtue.

- The pyramid signifies strength and duration: the eye over it and the motto allude to the many ways that providence has favored the American cause.

- The date underneath is that of the Declaration of Independence and the words under it (*novus ordo seclorum*) signify the beginning of the new American era, which commences from that date.

Now, unless Thomson was lying, this pretty much puts to rest the conspiracy theories . . . for now!

Lucky Numbers?

The right-hand circle on the back of the dollar bill is the seal of the president of the United States and it features the national bird, the bald eagle. Above the eagle, you have thirteen stars representing the thirteen original colonies. They say that the number 13 is an unlucky number. This is almost a worldwide belief. It is unusual to see a room numbered 13, or any hotels or motels with a 13th floor. But, think about this: 13 original colonies, 13 signers of the Declaration of Independence, 13 stripes on our flag, 13 steps on the pyramid, 13 letters in the Latin above, 13 letters in "*E pluribus unum*," 13 stars above the eagle, 13 plumes of feathers on each span of the eagle's wing, 13 bars on that shield, 13 leaves on the olive branch, 13 olives on the branch, and if you look closely, 13 arrows.

Yikes! All these thirteens on the dollar bill! How unlucky is that? Maybe that's why all these dollars keep vanishing from our pockets! (Or maybe we just keep finding things to spend them on).

In Bucks County, Pennsylvania, there's an old memorial garden that's now closed to the public. It used to be run by the Rosicrucians. The garden used to be a place where you could go for a walk among the . . . pyramids. There were two of them, and the big one had a room in it. You couldn't get in because there was a gate in front of it, but as you peeked in through the gate, you could see two very familiar circular designs on its walls: an unfinished pyramid topped with an eye and an eagle holding an olive branch and thirteen arrows. These are the seals on the back of the dollar bill. So why are they hidden inside a Rosicrucian pyramid? Is the Rosicrucian Order saluting the United States? Is it worshipping the mighty dollar? Or is our money actually branded with the seal of the Rosicrucians?

THE GHOSTS OF WAR

Chapter 9

Often at Weird Central, we share stories about class trips that we went on as kids. Fondly, we recall our outings to zoos and planetariums, but the class trips that we remember most vividly are visits to historic battlegrounds. Even though the sites we visited were different, our experiences were oddly similar, and all of us came away convinced that the places were haunted. Perhaps it was the chill in the air or the gloomy atmosphere, full of sadness and tragedy. Every day, we here at Weird Central get letters that describe strange happenings at America's historic battlegrounds. Some claim they've spotted the spirits of soldiers who don't know that the war is long over. Others insist that they've glimpsed wandering souls, eternally searching for loved ones who died in battle. Are these tales true? Read on and decide for yourself.

Ghosts of Gettysburg

The first time we took the Weirdmobile out to Gettysburg, Pennsylvania, we got lost. We parked and walked into a grocery store to ask for directions to the battlefield. The answer was not what we were expecting. "It's right here!" said the clerk. "Here?" we asked, gazing ahead at the crowded produce aisle. An old woman buying cat food helped us out. She explained that the Battle of Gettysburg was fought in fields, forests, and the streets of the town. In other words, the entire village was the battlefield.

The three-day-long clash was the turning point of the American Civil War—and its bloodiest moment. Ultimately, it was a victory for the North, but both sides suffered severe losses—7,500 soldiers died between July 1 and July 3, 1863, and more than 40,000 more were wounded—especially on the third day of the conflict. On that day, almost one-third of the men in combat were killed.

Today, Gettysburg National Military Park, the "official" battlefield of Gettysburg, is considered by many to be haunted. Several buildings that were used as hospitals are haunted, as is Gettysburg College. In fact, it seems as though all of Gettysburg is haunted. At least, that's what they say.

Has anyone seen my dog?

Our Weird colleague Troy Taylor wrote about the ghosts of Gettysburg in his book *Spirits of the Civil War*. He describes the strange smell of peppermint and vanilla wafting through the air on Baltimore Street. What do these odors have to do with hauntings? Taylor explains that, after the battle, when women walked through the streets, they would raise scented handkerchiefs to their faces to avoid the smell of decaying corpses. Are the hints of perfume on Baltimore Street actually "phantom smells" lingering from the distant past?

There's a triangular field in Gettysburg where cameras have been known to malfunction. Many frustrated photographers think that supernatural forces are to blame. And Gettysburg National Military Park is said to be inhabited by the restless spirits of both Confederate and Union soldiers. Sometimes they've been spotted marching in formation. Other times they've been seen attacking each other, fighting battles that will never end.

The Hummelbaugh House is supposedly haunted by the ghost of Confederate Brigadier General William Barksdale. Townspeople insist that on certain nights, you can hear the general's dying screams. And many believe that the Hummelbaugh Farm has a canine ghost as well. The story goes that the general's dog was so loyal, it refused to leave its master's grave. It died on the spot and returns to howl mournfully every year on July 2, the anniversary of the general's death.

But the oddest ghost legend of Gettysburg is also the oldest. It takes place while the battle was still raging. They say that a group of Union soldiers were lost and confused. But then a glowing apparition appeared. The spirit led the soldiers to a stronger position, where they were able to overpower a flank of Confederate men. Their victory helped win the battle, and the battle helped win the war. Afterward, the soldiers swore that the apparition looked an awful lot like George Washington.

With so many spooky stories to offer, it's no surprise that haunted Gettysburg has become a tourist destination for ghost hunters. Fortunately, they have plenty of ghost tours to choose from. One tour even offers every client a free EMF (electromagnetic frequency) meter, a device used by paranormalists to detect changes in magnetic fields. High readings are supposed to indicate that ghosts may be present. And some EMF meters have noise alerts to announce dramatic energy shifts. So, if you visit Gettysburg, don't be surprised if you encounter a few ghosts, or at least some tourists wandering about with loudly beeping ghost-o-meters.

Haunted Forts

Many battles have been won and lost in and around forts. And perhaps since they are permanent reminders of the past, ghosts tend to haunt the forts where their armies either won or lost. Check out some of these haunted forts.

The Alamo

The Alamo in San Antonio, Texas, is famous for its history *and* for its ghosts, and, to our knowledge, it's the only haunted fort that comes with a famous catchphrase: Remember the Alamo! The Alamo was originally built in the late 1700s as a mission, a place to convert Indians to Christianity. It was used as a burial ground between 1724 and 1793. Then, in 1836, it was the site of the bloody Battle of the Alamo. This was during the Texas Revolution, when American colonists in Texas were fighting for independence from Mexico. Using the Alamo as a fortress, approximately two hundred Texans held off thousands of Mexican soldiers for thirteen days.

Finally, the fortress fell and the rebellious Texans inside were killed. Ghosts have been spotted in the area ever since. Twice, Mexican troops were ordered to destroy the Alamo, and both times, soldiers claimed that spirits appeared to protect the fortress. "Do not touch the Alamo, do not touch these walls!" the ghosts warned. Terrified, the soldiers ran away and refused to return. In the late 1800s, the Alamo was used as a jail. The staff and prisoners complained of moaning sounds, phantom shadows, and eerie apparitions pacing the roof.

Today, the Alamo is one of the most popular destinations in Texas. Millions visit each year, and there are more weird sightings than ever. Tourists have reported seeing ghosts dancing along the outer walls, huddled in the barracks, and even roaming about in the gift shop. Some say that the fort is haunted by the ghost of a small blond boy searching for his father. "Remember the Alamo!" cried Sam Houston's Texan Army during the Battle of San Jacinto in 1836. It seems that a lot of ghosts have taken this advice to heart.

Fort Mifflin

In 1777 the British laid siege to Fort Mifflin, which stands on an island just south of Philadelphia. By taking the fort, the British were hoping to control the Delaware River and gain access to the colonists' supply ships. Then, with fresh supplies, they planned to mount an attack on George Washington's troops and win the war. The siege began in early October and continued for seven weeks. The British pounded away at the fort with an unceasing barrage of cannonballs (as many as a thousand rounds every twenty minutes!), but the defenders of the fort held on. Finally, Fort Mifflin fell, but by that time, it was mid-November and winter had arrived. It was too late for the British to carry out their plans.

The fort was restored later on, and then used as a prison during the Civil War. More recently, Fort Mifflin has been converted into a tourist attraction that's also a well-known destination for ghost hunters. Visitors say that on some nights, as the sun sets, if you look up toward the second-story balcony, you might be able to spot a figure carrying a long pole, lit on one end. It's the spirit of an old lamplighter, attending to his ghostly rounds. The casements of the fort are haunted by two shades known as the Faceless Man and the Screaming Lady. The Faceless Man is the ghost of a murderer named

Here's a detail of a photograph of a Civil War reenactment taken at Fort Mifflin in 1997 by Ray Morgenweck, using original photography equipment from the 1860s. If you look closely at the right side of the photo, just above the men, there appears to be a ghost image of a soldier not exactly standing on the ground.

William Howe, who was hanged at Fort Mifflin during the Civil War. In those days, prisoners were often executed with black bags over their heads. That's why you can't see Howe's ghostly face. The Screaming Lady is never seen, but her shrieking cries can be heard for miles (and have proven to be a frequent local disturbance). She's thought to be the spirit of Elisabeth Pratt, a sad soul who committed suicide after her daughter died of typhoid fever. Perhaps the most unsettling ghost of all is an undead guide, who has given extensive tours. So if you visit Fort Mifflin and you ask your tour guide if the place is haunted, don't be shocked if he turns to you and replies, "Yes, by me!"

Will someone ask the Screaming Lady to pipe down?

Fort de Chartres

Fort de Chartres, an old military outpost in Prairie du Rocher, Illinois, is home to one of the strangest recurring ghostly visitations in the world of weird: the Phantom July Fourth Funeral Procession. Townspeople claim that the event happens only when Independence Day falls on a Friday, and they insist that the spectral procession can only be seen if three bystanders position themselves by the side of the road near Fort de Chartres between 11 PM and midnight. Needless to say, there are so many rules surrounding this event that not many have actually seen it.

The first sighting happened on July 4, 1889. A woman named Mrs. Chris was sitting on her front porch, chatting with two friends, when they noticed movement in the street. The story goes that they looked up to find wagons passing by with soldiers strolling alongside on foot. Stranger still, the procession was entirely silent. As they watched breathlessly, Mrs. Chris and her friends heard nothing but the rustling of the trees. Forty wagons drifted past, followed by a low wagon bearing a casket. Some locals believe that the original funeral happened in the late 1700s. According to legend, a man had been murdered in a brawl and government officials didn't want news of the incident to spread. To prevent the funeral from attracting attention, they decided to conduct it at midnight.

Custer's Last Stand

As European settlements in the New World began to grow and multiply, and governments were formed, conflicts with Native American populations became more and more common. The ensuing battles, known as the Indian Wars, lasted until the late 1800s. The Battle of Little Bighorn got its name because it happened near the Little Bighorn River in eastern Montana. On the morning of June 25, 1876, General George Armstrong Custer was impatient to launch an attack against the Lakota Sioux and Northern Cheyenne Indians. Disobeying orders, he decided not to wait for reinforcements. Instead, he charged into battle with the U.S. Seventh Cavalry. Seven hundred men were split into three battalions, and each group rode into the Indian camp from a different direction. However, the camp was large—containing as many as 1,800 Native American warriors—and was led by Sitting Bull, who was well prepared for the attacks. The first two battalions were forced to retreat. Then, Custer led a surge of 210 men into the village. They were surrounded and killed in a bloody skirmish known as Custer's Last Stand.

If you visit Little Bighorn Battlefield in Big Horn County, Montana, you'll see a large granite memorial. Inscribed on it are the names of the cavalrymen who perished on that day. And surrounding it are small stones marking where each man died. One marker has a black background to help the letters stand out:

G.A. CUSTER BVT. MAJ. GEN. LT. COL. 7TH U.S. CAV. FELL HERE JUNE 25 1876

General Custer may have fallen near the marker, but he's been keeping busy ever since. Nighttime visitors to Little Bighorn National Park have seen the general inspecting the grounds. Other apparitions at Custer's Last Stand include phantom soldiers and Native American warriors, whooping and hollering, riding phantom horses.

Custer standing before his Last Stand.

Sitting Bull sitting.

Old Green Eyes and the Lady in White

In Tennessee, there's a stretch of untamed land, a dense forest area full of limestone boulders. Its name comes from the ancient Cherokee: Chickamauga, meaning the River of Death. Two historical battles took place at Chickamauga: one occurred during the War of 1812, and the other was the Battle of Chickamauga—one of the greatest Confederate victories during the American Civil War. In two days, from September 19 to September 20, 1863, thousands were killed and tens of thousands were wounded.

The battlegrounds are now part of Chickamauga National Military Park, a peaceful refuge for migrating birds and a popular attraction for Civil War enthusiasts. To remind us of darker times, the park also has some supernatural inhabitants. Workers have heard unearthly war cries at night and have spotted mysterious phantom soldiers. Other visitors have run into Old Green Eyes. Rumor has it that he was a Confederate soldier ripped apart by a cannonball. His head was found and buried, but his body was never located. Ever since then, Old Green Eyes has scoured the fields at night, searching in vain for his missing body. Another sad spirit of Chickamauga is a floating lady in white. She won't rest until she finds her boyfriend, but he died in the battle almost 150 years ago.

ANCIENT MYSTERIES

american history falls into two distinct parts: the bits that happened after Columbus discovered the continent, and the vast epochs that came before then. The pre-Columbian years are steeped in mystery, mostly because we can't rely on written accounts to tell us what happened. To figure it out, we have to examine whatever evidence we can find: stone structures in back woods, coded messages carved into stone, old folk stories, and more. Does that sound like a lot of effort? Well, it's not if you enjoy mysteries, and there are plenty of them in the ancient history of our continent.

I got here first!

Written in Stone

The year 1492 is the first recorded date in the history of the Americas. That was when Columbus discovered the continent. It took more than a century for Europeans to try to settle in the northern bit that we now call the United States. Before that, we just can't be sure of anything. We have lots of things in writing to help us, but they are carved into rocks in a mysterious language made up of pictures. They have an impressive-sounding name—*petroglyphs*, which means "something carved in rock." Nobody can agree on what many of these petroglyphs mean or even who carved them. Did ancient Native Americans carve these rocks or was it European visitors who came long before Columbus? These rocks are among history's greatest mysteries.

The Dighton Rock

If you look in history books about New England, you'll see the name Cotton Mather crop up a lot. He was a pastor and a prolific writer in the late 1600s who was probably best known for his involvement in the Salem Witch Trials. But he also wrote about other things he came across in Massachusetts, including a river rock with a strange story behind it.

Translation: *We got here first!*

In a book he wrote more than three hundred years ago called *The Wonderful Works of God Commemorated*, Mather mentioned a series of strange characters carved deep into a rock at the mouth of the Taunton River near the town of Dighton, Massachusetts. The inscription was ten feet wide and looked like a long string of doodles—but it was too well carved to be anything as silly as doodling. All Cotton Mather could say about it was that the strange symbols "suggest as odd Thoughts about them that were here before us, as there are odd Shapes in that Elaborate Monument." In other words—the shapes are weird, and so were the people who wrote them.

The Dighton Rock now resides in its very own museum, the Dighton Rock State Park.

Over the centuries, people have come up with lots of theories about the rock. A French count announced in 1781 that it was clearly written by sailors from ancient Carthage (on the coast of Africa). About twenty-five years later, a Harvard scholar named Samuel Harris declared that some of the lettering was Phoenician and he could read three Hebrew words in it: *King, Priest,* and *Idol*. And twenty-five years after that, a Maryland schoolteacher named Ira Hill declared that the inscription dated back to the reign of King Solomon and described an expedition from Tyre described in the Old Testament.

All of these explanations are pretty far-fetched, but that doesn't mean the real story isn't just as bizarre. After all, this rock is very carefully carved, with all the symbols facing the open water, not the land. So they were written for the benefit of sailors entering the river from the ocean. Who could be coming in from the North Atlantic before the Pilgrims, needing to read a strange set of squiggles on a rock?

One Danish scholar had the most well-researched answer of all. His name was Carl Christian Rafn, and after reading ancient Icelandic manuscripts, he made the connection between North America and three legendary lands that feature in Viking stories. The countries were called Helluland, Markland, and Vinland. The stories were set in about 1000 ACE and concerned a character called Leif the Lucky. A second set of sagas set seven years later mentioned a character called Thorfinn Karlsefni, who sailed along the coast of these far-flung lands to a place called Hop. We'll hear more about Thorfinn a bit later, but Carl Rafn believed that Hop was probably in what is now Massachusetts and Rhode Island.

So there's a lot more to this river rock in Massachusetts than meets the eye. But exactly how much more there is to it, we'll never know. It's as full of mystery now as it was in the days of the Salem Witch Trials.

Track Rock Gap

We're not ancient linguists or scholars of Native American hieroglyphics, but even we had no difficulty interpreting the petroglyphs carved on the boulders at Track Rock Gap in the Chattahoochee National Forest, near Blairsville, Georgia. The six soapstone boulders are covered with hundreds of symbols, each a faithful representation of animal tracks: horse hoofs, buffalo, deer, and rabbit tracks. There are also human footprints, in twenty-six different sizes.

One of the human footprints is huge even by basketball player standards—it's seventeen inches long and could belong only to a giant of Shaq O'Neal stature. (Actually, he'd be bigger than our basketball hero—Shaq's feet are only a bit more than sixteen inches long.)

Archaeologists speculate that the carvings were made anywhere from 3,000 to 10,000 years ago by the Cherokee Indians.

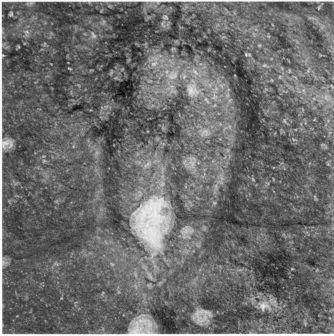

It's difficult to photograph the boulders since each is covered by a metal cage to protect the soft soapstone from tourists.

The Indian God

Massachusetts doesn't have a monopoly on river rocks with writing on them. About five miles due south of Franklin in Venango County, Pennsylvania, there's a rock on the left bank of the Allegheny River that's so impressive, they call it the Indian God. It was never worshipped by Native Americans, of course, but it's been famous for hundreds of years because of its huge size—twenty-two feet high—and its bizarre carvings. There are literally hundreds of them, including arrows, snakes, birds, hands, turtles, and what look like X-rays of humans. The old inscriptions are on the side facing the river; the side that faces the riverbank is full of tourist graffiti from the 1800s onwards.

The first Europeans to write about this out-of-the-way site were French voyagers who sailed down the river from Canada to claim land for France. A man named Blenville de Celeron buried a territorial marker next to the rock on August 3, 1749, and noted the location—"near a large stone on which are many figures crudely engraved."

In 1889, a fellow named R. W. Criswell compared the carvings on the Indian God rock to the ones on Dighton rock and came to the conclusion that both rocks were carved by the Viking hero Thorfinn Karlsefni.

Of course, this is a historic mystery, so one explanation is never enough! A famous scholar-adventurer from the 1800s named Henry Schoolcraft believed the rock was carved by native tribes. And he should know: he spent thirty years among the tribes of the Great Lakes region. With his great knowledge of Native American cultures, he had some very interesting insights into the carvings:

> *The inscription itself appears distinctly to record in symbols the triumphs of hunting and war. The bent bow and arrow are twice distinctly repeated. The arrow by itself is repeated several times. . . . The animals captured . . . are not deer or common game, but objects of higher triumph. There are two large panthers or cougars.*

So there you have it. A bona fide mystery rock, with two good explanations—and they can't both be right. If you're energetic, you can visit the Indian God Rock for yourself: just find your way to the Allegheny River Trail, and either cycle south from Franklin for about eight miles along the winding river or hike a couple of miles up from the river's edge at Brandon.

Old-fashioned graffiti on the riverbank side of the Indian God Rock.

The Judaculla Rock

In the mountains of Jackson County, North Carolina, stands a rock covered with carved lines, circles, stick figures, and doodles. This soapstone boulder is called the Judaculla Rock, and it takes its name from a mispronounced Cherokee word, *Tsul'Kalu'*, which is a legendary giant with slanted eyes. The legend has it that the giant's mother was a comet and his father was thunder, and he had seven fingers on each hand. One day, he scratched the boulder with his fingers or toes, and he accidentally created the mysterious markings.

We like seven-fingered legendary giants as much as the next person, but in the interests of being more historical, we decided to gather some other interpretations of the carvings on Judaculla Rock. To the untutored eye, these lines and circles look a bit like a map or perhaps a kind of Cherokee graphic novel that tells an old tribal story. But that's just a guess. A paranormal group based in Asheville, North Carolina, believes they may be pictures of microscopic organisms. Of course, this raises an obvious question: if this rock was carved thousands of years before microscopes were invented, how would the carvers know what microorganisms looked like? The group had a quick answer: thousands of years ago, space aliens came to North Carolina and covered the rock with squiggly etchings of microorganisms. Ooookay. Thanks for that one, guys. We're sticking with the tale of the seven-fingered giant for now. It doesn't seem so far-fetched anymore.

Towering Mystery

There's a tower in Newport, Rhode Island, that people have been calling "the old stone mill" for more than 350 years. It's shaped like the center of a toilet roll with arches at the bottom, and nobody's really sure where the tower came from or who built it.

One legend has it that the first colonial governor of Rhode Island, Benedict Arnold (not the Revolutionary War traitor but his great-grandfather), built the tower as a windmill in the 1600s. That's the normal story; however, many people believe it was never a mill and that Arnold had nothing to do with its construction. They say it may have been built by much earlier European explorers.

A Danish archaeologist named Carl Rafn said that the tower was remarkably similar to Viking churches and watchtowers. He had analyzed the strange writings on a rock near the tower and believed ancient Vikings carved the petroglyphs. These findings led Rafn and other historians to theorize that the Vikings were the first people to colonize North America, many hundreds of years before the Pilgrims landed at Plymouth, and these Vikings had built this tower.

Others say the arched circular design of the tower resembles defensive towers used in the Orkney Islands off the coast of Scotland. It also looks like Irish round churches. These buildings date back to the fourteenth century—so perhaps the Scots or the Irish were the first settlers in the area. But there's even more! Another theory states that the tower looks just like the washroom buildings attached to Cistercian monasteries. So perhaps monks sailed out in search of new people to convert to Christianity and set up shop in Rhode Island in the twelfth century—a full five hundred years before Benedict Arnold governed the colony.

Windmill or washroom?

So, tucked away on Aquidneck Island in the state of Rhode Island is a big old mystery that could have been a mill, a church, a tower, or a monastery washroom. It might be the product of the colonial English, seafaring Vikings, evangelical Irish, warlike Scots, or Cistercian monks.

Mysterious Mounds

When American settlers started heading west, they stumbled upon awesome man-made mounds of earth. They knew that burial mounds were common in northern Europe and Egypt, but for some reason, they did not believe that Native Americans had the same practice. They had all kinds of strange theories about why something so obviously from the Old World was right there in the newly minted United States. Eventually, in 1894, the Bureau of American Ethnology confirmed that artifacts from mounds in Illinois were definitely of Native American origin, and that settled the argument. But it did nothing to solve the mysteries beneath these big piles of dirt.

Cahokia Mounds

Near Collinsville, Illinois, lay the remains of a huge and bustling Native American city called Cahokia. But you would never believe that the mounds of earth that lie there were once the homes of tens of thousands of people.

The center of what used to be the town is now called Monk's Mound, and it's sixteen acres across with a staircase for easy access. At the top, archaeologists have uncovered pipes for tobacco rituals and copper ornaments shaped like birds and snakes. These sound like the kind of things that belong in sacred places, so this might have been some sort of temple.

But that's about all we do know about Cahokia. There are no records or local legends about an enormous ancient city in the area. The site seems to have been empty long before Europeans arrived in the area—but why? Sadly, we have no answers . . . only questions.

Gone but Not Forgotten

In Pennsylvania, we have one tale of a mound that contained evidence that Bradford County was once the home to horn-headed basketball players from long ago. Well . . . maybe they weren't basketball players, but they were tall enough to be. Back in the 1880s, three respected scholars unearthed human remains from a mound outside of Sayre. Or perhaps we should say, almost-human remains. These two sets of skeletons were more than seven feet tall, with strange horn-like bumps just above the eyebrows that stuck out a full two inches. The team that unearthed these included the state historian Dr. G. P. Donehoo and two professors—A. B. Skinner of the American Investigating Museum and W. P. Morehead of Phillips Academy in Andover.

But despite their impressive credentials, they botched the job. Somehow they managed to ship the bones to the wrong address, because they never arrived back in Philadelphia and have never been seen since. We're sad to report this, because there's nothing we'd enjoy more on our next trip to Philly than a museum visit to see almost fifteen feet of human remains with four legs, four arms, and four horns between them.

Serpent Mound

Mounds are not just for burying people and cities, though. Here at Weird Central, we've heard about mounds that are more like giant sculptures that you can really see only from the sky. Experts call this type of mound an effigy mound, and one of the best examples is in southern Ohio. It's called the Serpent Mound, and it lies in a crater in a fifty-four-acre park in Adams County. Yep, that's right—it's a mound shaped like a snake in a crater that was formed when a meteor crash-landed in Ohio thousands of years ago. What could be cooler than that?

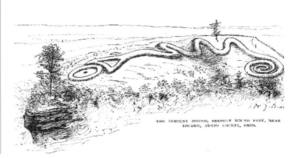

THE SERPENT MOUND, SERPENT MOUND PARK, NEAR LOCUST, ADAMS COUNTY, OHIO.

The snake is huge—about a quarter of a mile long from its mouth to its tail. The body curves gracefully through the grassy valley, from a spiral tail to a huge mouth, which lies wide open. It looks like it's about to swallow a giant egg. Or perhaps the body of a frog. Or maybe it's the sun. We can't quite tell, but whatever it is, the snake looks very hungry.

The best thing about the Snake Mound, of course, is the show-and-tell speech you can give after you visit it. When your teacher or your friends ask what you did on your vacation, you can tell them, "I went to see a 1,330-foot-long prehistoric serpent in a giant meteorite impact crater." And nobody could accuse you of making up stories. It's all true!

America's Stonehenge

Everybody's heard about Stonehenge. It's one of England's greatest ancient mysteries. But what's that got to do with American history and its mysteries? Well, nothing, actually, except for the fact that America has its own Stonehenge. It stands on top of a granite hilltop in Salem, New Hampshire, looking like the ancient abandoned rock village that it probably was.

Like the Stonehenge on England's Salisbury Plain, America's Stonehenge is a megalithic structure—that's another way of saying it's a bunch of large rocks made into something by humans. Also like England's glory, America's Stonehenge could be more than four thousand years old. It was discovered quite recently, though, in 1826.

A farmer climbed the hill and discovered a massive network of stone chambers and underground tunnels, all obviously made by hand—and some kind of machinery, too. Some of the stones are gigantic, weighing up to eleven tons, so it was clearly not just hauled into place on a whim. Most experts believe that the site was the work of prehistoric Native Americans, probably the ancestors of the Pennacooks of New Hampshire. But like every mystery we've uncovered so far, there are plenty of other explanations. Some other possibilities include traveling monks from Ireland, Celtic explorers, and Phoenicians.

But why would anyone build such a strange structure on a hill in New Hampshire? It's obvious that the site had been carefully laid out so that it could be used as an observatory for solar and lunar events. Most ancient structures in Europe and South and Central America seem to have been designed to work as some kind of calendar. But did it have other uses? Did people once live here? Or was it designed for some kind of ancient religious ceremony?

This granite table could have been a cutting board for food . . . or for human sacrifices!

A granite table on the ground seems like it could have been a "sacrificial stone." A gutter had been carved around the edge. Was this groove made so that sacrificial blood would drain off properly? Or was the table an ancient cutting board used in food preparation? One of our favorite archaeologists, an Englishwoman named Lucy Harrison, gave us some great insights into megalithic structures across the world, and they fit America's Stonehenge as well as any other "henge" you might have heard of. "They're not necessarily sacred

sites; they may just be gathering places," Lucy told us. "One word that archaeologists use a lot is *ritual*, but ritual is not just going to church on a Sunday. Ritual is also going to market on a Saturday morning; ritual is what you do for birthdays, what you do for Christmas. It's about life events, births, deaths, marriages. It's probably about healing. It's about social interaction, like gathering at a local shopping mall."

So maybe America's Stonehenge is a four-thousand-year old church, social center, and shopping mall all rolled into one. But whatever it was, you realize that today it's probably got the wrong name. Back when it was first discovered, people used to call it Mystery Hill. We think that's a pretty accurate description.

CEMETERY STORIES

In history class, you read about the lives of important historical figures. That's all well and good, but in some cases there's a lot of interesting material that's being left out, such as: what happened to them after they died? It sounds like a silly question, but some legendary characters from American history have death stories that are almost as intriguing as their life stories. And most times, you can begin your quest for information with the words written on the stones that mark their graves.

The Lincoln Tomb State Historic Site at Oak Ridge Cemetery, Springfield, Illinois.

Everything okay down there?

The Busy Afterlife of Abraham Lincoln

The story of Abraham Lincoln's life ended with his assassination in April 1865. The story of his death continued on for another forty-five years, and some believe that it continues to this day. Tragedy was nothing new to the Lincoln family. The president and his wife suffered through the death of their three-year-old son Eddie in 1850. Then in 1862, their son Willie passed away at the age of eleven. On May 4, 1865, a few weeks after the assassination, the bodies of Abraham Lincoln and his son Willie arrived at Oak Ridge Cemetery, not far from Springfield, Illinois. Soon, the two corpses were joined by a third. The body of Lincoln's son Eddie was unearthed from a nearby cemetery and also brought to Oak Ridge. A monument was under construction, and the three Lincolns were going to be laid to rest together as soon as it was finished.

The cadavers were put in a temporary tomb, but beforehand some of Lincoln's friends came up with a strange request. They wanted to check on the body to ensure that it was safe. A young plumber's assistant, Leon P. Hopkins, cut a hole in the lead coffin and peeked inside. The face of the corpse had been whitened with chalk to make it more presentable for viewings. Leon Hopkins gazed upon the unnaturally bright face and he gave the word that the body of Abraham Lincoln was fine. Then he re-covered the hole in the coffin and welded it shut.

From there, the story of Abraham Lincoln gets very complicated. On October 9, 1874, the monument was finished and the bodies were placed in a marble sarcophagus within the catacombs. A couple of years later, a band of grave robbers attempted to steal the remains, but their plan was foiled. Afterward, to protect the corpse, the custodian of Oak Ridge hid Lincoln somewhere in the halls of the building between the catacombs and the monuments. Over time, the deceased president was moved and moved again, and repeatedly Leon P. Hopkins was asked to check inside the coffin to make sure that the corpse was okay.

Finally, in 1901, at the request of Abraham Lincoln's surviving son, Robert, the casket was placed in a steel cage. The steel cage was lowered into a ten-foot hole and the hole was filled with concrete. However, some conspiracy theorists are convinced that the casket encased in cement was empty. They insist that the burial was a hoax devised by Robert Lincoln to protect his father's body by hiding its whereabouts. End of story? Not necessarily . . . The staff of Oak Ridge have heard footsteps and voices. And the apparition of Abraham Lincoln has been spotted nearby in Springfield. Perhaps even the ghost of the former president is confused by the weird happenings at Oak Ridge.

The Lincoln Special.

Lincoln's remains even had a long journey getting to their resting place. The body traveled 1,654 miles from Washington, D.C., to Springfield, Illinois, over thirteen days on a train dubbed "The Lincoln Special." The train traveled through 180 cities and seven states and made several stops along the way. Tens of thousands of mourners gathered along the tracks to witness the funeral train, and at each stop, the coffin was taken off the train, placed on a horse-drawn hearse, and led to a building for viewing. Accompanying Lincoln's body were the remains of his son Willie, which had been disinterred shortly after Lincoln's death so he could be buried with his father.

Jesse James

Three separate towns claim to have the body of the notorious outlaw Jesse James. This, of course, is two too many. The town most likely to have Jesse is Kearney, Missouri. James grew up in Kearney. The son of a preacher, he rebelled and never stopped rebelling. With his band of thieves, known as the James Gang, he rode through the Midwest robbing and killing. On April 3, 1882, at the age of thirty-four, Jesse James was shot in the back by one of his own men, Bob Ford, who was eager to collect a $10,000 reward for killing his cohort.

A monument to Jesse James in Kearney reads: "Murdered by a traitor and a coward whose name is not worthy to appear here." In nearby Mount Olivet Cemetery, there's a headstone with Jesse James's name and epitaph: "Born Sept. 5, 1847 Assassinated April 3, 1882." Yet, not everyone believes that it's actually James's body lying below the bandit's tombstone. Some claim that it's another member of the James Gang. The theory is that James conspired with Ford to fake his own death. Then, he hightailed it out of town to freedom. This brings us to the other two resting places of Jesse James, two towns in North Texas: Blevins and Granbury.

Depending on whom in Texas you speak with, after fleeing Missouri, Jesse James died either in Blevins at the age of 95 or in Granbury at the age of 103. In Texas, he supposedly used different assumed names to conceal his identity. For some, he was J. W. Gates. Others knew him as J. Frank Dalton. The legend goes that, near the end of his life, Dalton sat down with the Granbury sheriff and revealed the "truth," describing in great detail his criminal past as the infamous Jesse James.

Where is the real Jesse James buried? In recent years, scientists have attempted to unravel this mystery. DNA tests have indicated that the corpse in Kearney is a possible contender. But folks in Blevins and Granbury have disputed the evidence, which leaves us with three grave sites and no answers.

The Jesse James monument in Kearney—he's not buried here!

Is he here?

Here?

Or here?

Life Imprisonment

He was most likely born in New York City in 1859 under the name of Henry McCarty (though some people claim his real name was Henry Antrim), but when he died twenty-one years later, he was one of the most famous outlaws of the Wild West and had a completely different name: Billy the Kid. You can see his grave in Fort Sumner, New Mexico—in fact, you can't miss it. It's the grave that's completely surrounded by a cage! Billy the Kid escaped from jail lots of times when he was alive; now that he's buried, it looks like the lawmen aren't taking any chances.

When he was a teenager, Henry McCarty had to move to New Mexico when his mom got sick. She needed to live in a hot, dry climate to help her breathe, but the move came too late: she died there while Henry was still in his teens. Young Henry went off the rails after that. He was caught stealing laundry and ran away to avoid getting into trouble for his crime. While on the run, he got into an argument with a blacksmith and shot the older man dead. Although he was arrested, he broke out of jail and took on a new name, William Bonney, to keep the law off his trail. He soon joined a gang and shot more people, including a sheriff.

As William Bonney, he gained a reputation for being the most dangerous man in the Wild West, even though he wasn't yet twenty. The nickname Billy the Kid appeared soon after. He was caught in 1881, put on trial, and sentenced to hang. Before the sentence could be carried out, he escaped from jail. It took the local sheriff, Pat Garrett, three more months to track down the Kid. He shot him to death in July 1881. The Kid is buried between two of his companions who died the previous year—their graves marked with a single stone. The real reason that the grave is caged up has nothing to do with the three being jailbirds, though. It turns out that other criminals used to visit the spot and steal the gravestone. The cemetery got tired of replacing it, so they put the gravestone behind bars . . . in protective custody!

You best leave my gravestone be!

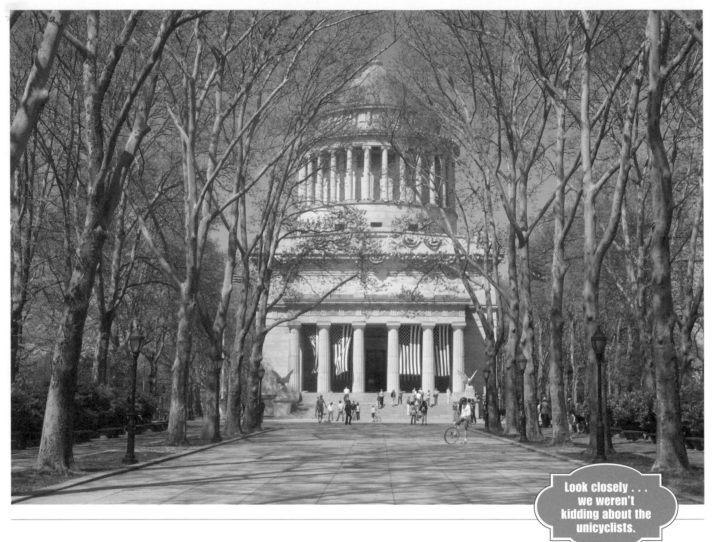

Look closely . . . we weren't kidding about the unicyclists.

Who's Buried in Grant's Tomb?

Ulysses S. Grant was the eighteenth president of the United States and the commanding general for the North during the Civil War. After he died in 1885, a monument in his honor was built in New York City. Eight thousand tons of granite were used in the tomb's construction. Finished in 1897, Grant's Tomb was—and still is—the biggest mausoleum in North America. On the day it opened, there was a parade of sixty thousand marchers, and more than a million people came to Riverside Park to watch. In the early part of the twentieth century, it was a huge tourist attraction that was more popular than the Statue of Liberty. So, what's weird about Grant's Tomb? Besides the ghost soldiers lurking about and the weird attraction unicyclists have for the place, this once popular attraction is now known mainly because of the trivia question, "Who's buried in Grant's tomb?"

In the 1950s, Groucho Marx, a comedian and one of the zany Marx Brothers, was the host of a game show called *You Bet Your Life*. He would always give contestants one question that was so easy they couldn't possibly get it wrong (What color is an orange?). Of all of his giveaway questions, the most famous was, "Who's buried in Grant's tomb?" And this nonsense question is still asked repeatedly today. The question is entered as a Google search about a thousand times per month. (In comparison, the nonsense question, "What's the number for 911?" is entered only about thirty-six times per month.)

Of course there are three acceptable answers to this question:

- Okay answer: Ulysses S. Grant
- Better answer: Ulysses S. Grant and his wife, Julia
- Best answer: No one. Grant and his wife share an aboveground sarcophagus, so technically they're not buried.

Buried Body Parts of the Old South

ARM OF STONEWALL JACKSON MAY 3, 1863.

On the Confederate side of the Civil War, no general except for Robert E. Lee commanded more respect than Thomas "Stonewall" Jackson. He earned that nickname because he held back the Union forces at Bull Run like a stone wall. It was unfortunate, then, that the general's left arm was shattered in early May 1863 by what is called "friendly fire"—an accidental shot from someone on his own side. Seeing no hope of mending the wounds, field doctors amputated his arm and hoped for the best. Sadly for the Confederacy, Stonewall Jackson died eight days later. If you go to the battleground at Chancellorsville, Virginia, you can see a large obelisk that marks the spot where Stonewall was shot, as well as the final resting place for his arm. It was buried in a steel box in the Wilderness Battlefield. The date on the stone, May 3, 1863, was a week before the general died but the day on which his arm was removed. Stonewall Jackson's grave is in Lexington, Virginia.

Houdini's Halloween

Harry Houdini was a world-renowned magician and possibly the greatest escape artist who ever lived. Handcuffs, water-filled tanks, steamer trunks . . . nothing could hold Houdini for long. He could free himself from straitjackets with ease, even while dangling upside down from a crane.

If you've heard about Houdini, chances are that you've heard about how he passed away. A student named J. Gordon Whitehead punched him in the stomach as a challenge to test the magician's strength. Nine days later, Houdini died from a ruptured appendix. Nowadays, doctors doubt that the punches caused Houdini's death. They insist that the magician had appendicitis long before he met J. Gordon Whitehead. However, most people like the story of "the punchy student who killed the Great Houdini," so the tale has been passed down over time.

Houdini died on October 31, 1926. Many people think it's strange that the world's greatest magician passed away on Halloween. Another weird tidbit: he was buried in an airtight bronze coffin that he used in his act. During a performance just before his death, he had been locked in the casket underwater for an hour. Of course, at the time, he had no idea that he would soon be locked in it again . . . this time for good. Still, the freakiest aspect about Houdini's death is the fact that many people still expect him to perform one last stunt. They're waiting for him to send a message from beyond the grave.

Harry Houdini and his wife, Bess.

The Official Houdini Séance has been held every Halloween for more than eighty years. To our knowledge, while Bess was alive no medium ever gave her the code. So it seems that no one has ever successfully channeled the spirit of Houdini. Before she died, Bess revealed the secret code to the public:

*Rosabelle * Answer * Tell * Pray Answer * Look. * Tell * Answer Answer * Tell*

The word *Rosabelle* was engraved inside Bess's wedding band. It was the title of a song that she used to sing, and the word had become Houdini's favorite nickname for his wife.

The rest of the message might seem like gibberish, but magicians recognize it as a code used by mentalists to secretly communicate with their assistants during mind-reading acts. In this weird magic language, Houdini's code spelled out a word:

B-E-L-I-E-V-E!

Houdini's grave is in the Machpelah Cemetery in Queens, New York. Every year near Halloween, the Society of American Magicians meets there and pays tribute to Harry Houdini by breaking a wooden wand over the tomb. The meaning is clear: what good is a magic wand without a great magician to wave it?

While Houdini was alive, he worked tirelessly to expose mediums as frauds. He even came up with a plan to debunk phony spiritualists after his death. He chose ten words and gave them to his wife, Bess. He instructed her to attend annual séances. If the medium was able to give the secret code, then Bess would know that Houdini was attempting to communicate with her from the spirit world.

Old Drum

Sniff, sniff . . . We get choked up every time someone mentions Old Drum. Old Drum wasn't as accomplished a dog as Jim the Wonder Dog (see page 52), and perhaps he doesn't belong here with the history makers in this chapter; however, his unfortunate death gave rise to a popular saying, so that's good enough for us!

As we've said, Old Drum's life achievements won't go down in dog history. But his death in 1869 created a very big fuss. Old Drum was a hound dog who loved to go hunting with his owner, Charles Burden. They lived together on a farm near Kingsville, Missouri, beside the home of Burden's brother-in-law, Leonidas Hornsby. Hornsby was also a farmer, and his livestock had often been attacked by wolves. Fed up, he decided to take action.

One day, Old Drum wandered onto Hornsby's property and was shot by Hornsby. The shooting led to a long court battle between Charles Burden and his brother-in-law. Burden's lawyer was a dog lover named George G. Vest. During the proceedings, Vest read a now-famous speech called "Eulogy of the Dog." There's a monument to Old Drum near the creek where his body was found. Another memorial in Warrensburg, Missouri, has a statue of Old Drum frozen in a classic "hunting dog" pose. Beneath the statue is a plaque. Engraved on it is the "Eulogy of the Dog," which contains the words that gave birth to the phrase "dog is man's best friend."

"The one absolutely unselfish friend that a man can have in this selfish world, the one that never deserts him, the one that never proves ungrateful or treacherous, is the dog."

Sniff, sniff

Acknowledgments

Matt Lake:

I know that without John Lake, Chris Lake, and Arnold Toynbee I wouldn't be nearly as excited about history as I am. And without Julia, Nicole, Danny, Stephan, and Genea reminding me that I myself qualify as a historical artifact, I'd have less of a sense of humor about it. And without the Marks, I'd never have considered history as weird as it truly is. Thanks to all of you!

Randy Fairbanks:

I'm grateful to all of the aficionados of weirdness who helped on this book. Mark Moran and Mark Sceurman guided us with ever-watchful weird eyes. Matt Lake is a wonderful writer and a big fan of Benjamin Franklin and of all things bizarre—the perfect partner for a book on Weird U.S. history. I'm glad I've had the opportunity to work with him. Thanks to our editor, Joe Rhaligan, for keeping the book tight, focused, and fun, and to the many unsung heroes behind this book: the contributors to *Weird U.S.* who have compiled a vast and indispensable archive of oddities. Also to my wife, Elizabeth Applegate, for her comments, encouragement, and funny dances. (Benjamin Franklin's toga-sporting, dancing ghost should take notes!) Special thanks to librarian Laura Follmer and to the kids at Goodnoe. My annual visits to your school help keep me writing. Stay weird!

INDEX

About Weird US

Weird U.S. is Mark Moran and Mark Sceurman, otherwise known as "The Marks." A long, long time ago, they started collecting weird stories about their home state of New Jersey and publishing them in a cool little pamphlet called Weird N.J. It wasn't long before they were gathering weird stories from every corner of the state. That led to the publication in 2003 of their bestselling *Weird N.J.: Your Travel Guide to New Jersey's Local Legends and Best Kept Secrets.* Soon people from all over the U.S. were sending the Marks strange stories, and that's how Weird U.S. came to be. The Marks have authored and/or published dozens of *Weird* books over the years and even starred in their own TV show. So, you may be wondering, how does the Weird U.S. staff decipher the fact from the fiction? How do they separate the history from the mystery? They don't. What they do is listen to what people tell them is weird about their own hometown. They collect these stories and try, wherever possible, to corroborate these seemingly fantastic tales with actual events and historical data. Sometimes they are successful and manage to uncover a little known tidbit of historical validity, and sometimes they don't. If they find that a local legend is patently untrue, do they refrain from publishing it? Absolutely NOT, if it's a great story! So how will you, the reader, know which stories are real and which are imagined, and where to draw the line between fact and fantasy? That's for you to decide. Weird U.S. merely presents these local legends to you in the most unadulterated form possible for you to ponder. One thing the folks at Weird U.S. will tell you though: none of the stories in this book are fiction—some might not be completely true, but none were made up solely for the purpose of entertainment.

About the Authors

Matt Lake and Randy Fairbanks work for Weird U.S., investigating weirdness wherever they go and writing books for the mysterious Marks. Matt Lake has lived and worked in the first, second, and fourth largest cities in England, and in such diverse states as California, Pennsylvania, and Maryland. His writing and photography have appeared in the *New York Times, the San Francisco Chronicle, the Baltimore Sun*, and the Weird U.S. book series. Matt's last known address was the driver's seat of a black car heading across the Conowingo Dam, shrouded in an early morning mist. Randy Fairbanks grew up in Stanhope, New Jersey, and spent far too much time in the woods hunting for imaginary creatures. After moving to New York, he became a filmmaker and a writer of children's stories. "Uncle Randy's Story Minute" was a popular feature of the weekly radio program *Greasy Kid Stuff* on WFMU. Randy lives in Brooklyn with his wife, and occasionally they go monster hunting together in Prospect Park.

Photo Credits

Page 5 Library of Congress; 6 Shutterstock; 7 top and middle Shutterstock, bottom Library of Congress; 8 left Shutterstock, right Library of Congress; 9 Library of Congress; 10 Ryan Doan/www.RyanDoan.com, (frame) Shutterstock; 11 Library of Congress; 12 left Library of Congress, right Shutterstock; 14 Library of Congress; 15 Library of Congress; 16 Library of Congress; 17 left © Andrew Balet, right Library of Congress; 18 Library of Congress; 19 left © Shawn Cummings/iStock, right © Damir Spanic/iStock; 20 top Library of Congress, bottom © Cristian Ioja; 21 top Library of Congress, bottom © Cristian Ioja; 22–23 Library of Congress; 24 Library of Congress; 25 © Les Byerley/iStock; 26 © Robert Dodge/iStock; 27 Shutterstock; 28–29 Library of Congress; 30 top Ryan Doan, bottom Library of Congress; 31 top Ryan Doan, bottom Library of Congress; 32 Library of Congress; 33 Ryan Doan; 34 Library of Congress, 35 top © Michael Stephens, bottom Library of Congress; 36 left Library of Congress, right © Daniel ter-Nedden & Carola Schibli/ghosttowngallery.com; 37–38 Library of Congress; 39 Joseph Citro; 40–41 Library of Congress; 42 Matt Lake; 43 Library of Congress; 44 Library of Congress; 45–48 Library of Congress; 49 Courtesy of Arizona Historical Society/Tuscon (AHS# 43892); 50–51 Ryan Doan; 52 © Robin Woltman; 53–54 Library of Congress; 55 Jeff Bellanger; 56 Matt Lake; 57 top Mark Moran, bottom Shutterstock; 58 Library of Congress; 59 Library of Congress; 60 left Matt Lake; 61 Library of Congress; 62 center and bottom © Jayson Kowinsky/www.fossilguy.com; 63 Joe Citro; 64 left Library of Congress, right Matt Lake; 65 Matt Lake; 66 Library of Congress; 67 Library of Congress; 68–70 Library of Congress; 71 top courtesy of John Smolenyak, center Mark Moran, bottom Rich Robinson; 72 Library of Congress; 73 left and right Ryan Doan; 74 bottom Mark Moran; 75 left and right Library of Congress, bottom Shutterstock; 76 Library of Congress; 77 top Library of Congress, bottom Jeff Belanger; 78–79 Jeff Belanger; 80 Library of Congress; 81 top Ryan Doan, bottom Library of Congress; 82 top Matt Lake, bottom Ryan Doan; 83 top and bottom © Timothy Renner; 84–85 Shutterstock; 86–87 Chris Gethard; 88 top Library of Congress; bottom Chris Gethard; 89 NASA; 90 Matt Lake; 91 top left and bottom right Joe Oesterle, bottom left Shutterstock; 92 top Shutterstock, bottom © Rob Johnson; 93–94 Shutterstock; 95 bottom two photos Matt Lake; 96 Library of Congress; 97 Library of Congress; 98 top © Eric Foltz/iStock, bottom © Greg Cooksey/iStock; 99 top © Samuel Kessler/iStock, bottom Library of Congress; 100 bottom courtesy Ray Morgenweck; 101 top Ryan Doan, middle Library of Congress, bottom Troy Taylor; 102–104 Library of Congress; 105 top Library of Congress, bottom Jeff Belanger; 106 © Alan Cressler; 107 Matt Lake; 108 © Kim Childrey; 109 Joe Citro; 110 © Skubasteve 834; 111 Library of Congress, 112–113 Mark Moran; 114 top Troy Taylor, bottom Library of Congress; 115 Library of Congress; 116 left Library of Congress, right top two James Strait, bottom two Wesley Treat; 117 top Eixo, bottom Library of Congress; 118 Shutterstock; 119 left Library of Congress, right Mark Moran; 120 Library of Congress, 121 right Anthony; 122 top en.wikipeia, bottom Abernaki.

SHOW US YOUR WEIRD!

Do you know of a weird site found somewhere in the U.S., or can you tell us about a strange experience you've had? If so, we'd like to hear about it! We believe that every town has at least one great tale to tell, and we're listening. It could be a cursed road, a haunted grocery store, an odd character, or a bizarre historic event. In most cases, these tales are told only in the towns in which they originated. But why keep them to yourself when you could share them with all of America? So come on and fill us in on all the weirdness that's lurking in your backyard!

You can e-mail us at: editor@weirdUS.com

Or write to us at:
Weird U.S., P.O. Box 1346
Bloomfield, NJ 07003
www.weirdus.com

Hey, you can also join our club for kids:
www.weirdclub.com